UNLOCK YOUR MIND
UNLOCK YOUR MONEY

Stop Admiring The Wealthy
And Become ONE!

SAMUEL & GEORGIA,

IT WAS A PLEASURE MEETING BOTH OF YOU. I HOPE AND PRAY GOD WILL USE BOTH OF YOU TO CHANGE THE LIVES OF MILLIONS.

THANKS FOR YOUR SUPPORT

DERRICK J. LOVE

Published by Derrick J. Love
Copyright © 2013 by Derrick J. Love. All rights reserved.

Unlock Your Mind...Unlock Your Money
ISBN:978-0-9891941-0-5

713-575-LOVE (5683)
Email: info@derrickjlove.com
www.facebook.com/unlockyourmoney
www.derrickjlove.com

Printed in the United States of America.

Cover Design: Edward Martinez
Book Production: Marvin D. Cloud, mybestseller Publishing Company.
marvindcloud@marvindcloud.com

Praise for
Unlock Your Mind, Unlock Your Money

"Clear, precise, practical and easy to read with step-by-step instructions... it doesn't get any more basic than this. If you are looking for a user-friendly guide to help you turn your money around, whether you are sixteen or sixty years old, this is it!"
– Samuel Johnson, CPA,
Financial Advisor

"Love is masterful in capturing the essence of the desperate financial state in which we Americans live and empowering us with what it takes to move from that place to one of financial success. He understands why we are where we are and helps us get to where we want to go! Thank you, Mr. Love, for this wonderful gift!"
– Angelic D. Chaison, Ph.D

"A brilliant mix of practicality, functionality, spirituality and entertainment, all rolled into a masterful presentation of why it is especially important to Christians to get their financial houses in order. Exceptional!"
– Shannon Williams, Ph.D.

"Who knew a financial book could offer such insight into my mentality, and the obstacles I've faced? It's like Derrick was talking directly to me as I was reading this book. Awesome job!"
—Simone Richardson

UNLOCK YOUR MIND
UNLOCK YOUR MONEY

Dedication

I would like to dedicate this book to a very special person in my life and that person is none other than YOU! Regardless of how you came into contact with this book, having it in your hands is not a coincidence. This is a divine encounter and there's something in it for you that will help you on your journey. If you are reading this book, then you've probably experienced some financial frustrations at some point in your life, and you may even be dealing with a financial struggle right now.

As I struggled financially, I sought many financial books to teach me how to improve my financial situation, but after many "ah hah," moments, I was still void of substance and practical ways to fix my problem. My motivation for writing this book was to provide a reliable and workable alternative to a better financial life for you and others who may be frustrated with their finances and feel that there is no way of escape. I've poured out my life into this book with hopes that my story and the lessons I've learned will motivate and encourage you to change your financial life and ultimately to pursue your God-intended life.

Acknowledgments

I've heard people say "behind every good man is a good woman," and I can truly say I agree with that statement. God Himself even said, "he who finds a wife finds a good thing." I would not be able to do what I do without the support and encouragement of my wife, Cawana Love, by my side. She makes me feel like I can accomplish anything I set my mind to. She has been a tremendous wife and friend to me for over a decade, and I feel like we're just getting started on our lifelong journey. Marriage is not the place to seek happiness, however having her on my side makes marriage enjoyable. She has been an excellent partner with helping to raise our two children, Derrick J Love, II, and London A. Love.

Behind every good student there is an excellent Master Teacher. I would like to honor my spiritual father, Apostle Dana Carson who is the ultimate model of what living a God focused life should look like. He is truly a leader that I look to for guidance for both spiritual and natural wisdom. He has been influential in my life for over ten years, and I would not be the man I am today if it wasn't for his leadership, mentorship and discipleship. He constantly stretches me beyond my comfort zone, and challenges me to go beyond the limitations of my own mind. Apostle

Carson is truly a (my) gift from God sent to shape and mold me into the person God created me to be. His relentless pursuit of God makes it virtually impossible for anyone under his leadership to settle for "that'll do." Several years ago we were having a conversation about finances and he told me I should write a book. Because of the office he holds in God's Kingdom, I acted on his authority and started writing. As a result of those words spoken, I was encouraged to write this book. Thank you Apostle!

There are many other people that have been influential in helping me to develop into the man I've become today. However, I'm not going to attempt to name all of them because inevitably someone will be forgotten due to my occasional memory lapse. In order to prevent any misunderstandings, I will just say thanks to all of my family and friends for supporting and encouraging me in this endeavor.

CONTENTS

Foreword

There comes a defining moment in all of our lives when we are faced with a moment of truth – a pivotal turning point that could mean the difference between realizing a great destiny or continuing to live a life of status quo. This moment, if not seized, could either be the moment wherein we look back twenty years later, reflecting on what could have been or the moment to which we refer as the day that we were bold and courageous enough to seize the opportunity of a lifetime to go to the next level. This, my friends, is called the moment of truth.

It is unfortunate that many of us do not realize the true extent of how much our mentalities have to do with where we are in life today. Like it or not, you are where you are because of how you think—our decisions determine our direction and our mentalities determine our manifestations. Though many people do not like where they are and the condition of the lives they lead, they fail to make the connection to the condition of their lives, the mentalities that got them there, and the decisions that they actively make on a daily basis to keep them there. This is especially true concerning our shaky financial conditions: while we have no appreciation for the state of our financial houses, the daily choices that we make keep us locked in them as virtual prisoners.

Struggling to live from paycheck to paycheck is complicated, challenging, stressful and difficult, and yet every single day, because our mentalities and our choices do not change, neither do our situations. The key to changing your financial condition is not in a magic formula. It is not in earning another college degree or gaining more intelligence. It is not in relinquishing all control of your money to be managed by the most frugal person in the family. It is not in clipping more coupons or finding more sales. The key to changing your financial condition is in renewing your mind about what it takes to operate as wise financial stewards. Only with a changed mind will you change your actions and set yourself on a journey towards financial success.

Unlock Your Mind, Unlock Your Money presents its readers with clear and practical, yet critical keys that are vital to transforming the mind into one that thinks properly about personal money management. While these keys are not difficult to understand, embracing them and implementing them will require a great deal of discipline. In reading the book, you will be encouraged to toss out your old way of thinking about money to make room for these new ideas that are designed to <u>completely</u> change the way you think about, relate to and handle money.

At the end of the book, not only will you be empowered with easy-to-understand steps and keys that will unlock your mind, you will be inspired to actually put them into action! You will say to yourself, "I think I can *really* do this!"

Reading this book will be your moment of truth. It is the moment of a lifetime in which you will be challenged to face where you are, how you got there, and what it takes to get out of this place of bondage and move to a new place called "financial freedom." Will you seize the moment? Will you allow this to be "the day that everything changed," the day marked by going from living with a consumer mentality to living with a healthy money mentality? Will this be the day that you will say goodbye to the stresses of living in a fragile financial state to living in the joyful world of financial freedom? The choice is up to you.

I encourage you to take out your calendar and a pen, and place a big circle around today's date. Why? Because this will go down as the day in your personal history that *everything* in your world changed! If you are perceptive enough, if you are open enough, if you are fed up enough with living below where God wants you to be as a financial steward, and if you are bold and courageous enough to set out on the journey, this will be that day for you – a day that you will always remember. If not, perhaps the day will come in which you will no longer tolerate living in financial bondage, and you will remember the principles that you have read in this book and return to them for your mental liberation. In either case, seize the moment. Seize the day. Seize your mentality, and seize your money!

Much success in your journey,

Paul Cox,
Lending and Equity Officer

Introduction

If you're like most people in this world, what you have is never enough, and by "what you have," I mean "money"-aka "cheddar," "benjamins," "dolla bills," the ''greenback,'' etc. We seem to never have enough of it. Most of our mental energies, daydreams and sleepless nights are spent trying to figure out how to get more of it. We spend countless hours envisioning what life would be like if we had an unlimited supply of money. Our dreams and fantasies of living a life of luxury is what allows *get rich quick* vehicles like the lottery to be sustained in any economy.

Regardless of race, class or gender, money motivates and inspires people like nothing else in life. Say what you will, but money is powerful! It can be the impetus for working over 80 hours per week, choosing to work overtime versus going to your kid's sporting events, and even compromising ourselves and the values for which we stand.

Back in the 1970's, the O'Jays dominated the pop charts with their hit song, "For the Love of Money" in which they described how people would steal from their mother, rob their own brother, and do "bad thangs" like cheat, lie, and even kill – all for the love of money. It's no secret that the desire for money has caused people to do all sorts of evil deeds in pursuit of accumulating more of this "magical paper." Nonetheless, be not deceived! Money in and of itself is NOT the enemy! Money is simply the motivating factor that causes the inner YOU to manifest.

When we examine a capitalistic society that is motivated and driven by the accumulation of money and material things, there seems to be a disconnection between those who actually achieve their financial dreams and the rest of us who only dream about achieving ours. I've often wondered what allows some people to maximize their efforts when it comes to wealth building, while others seem to have a difficult time meeting their basic needs. If you're like me, perhaps you've wondered about this, too.

Have you ever attempted to increase your income, thinking that a pay raise or large bonus would be the break you needed to achieve financial freedom, only to realize shortly after receiving the extra money that you were right back in the same situation? If you've experienced this before, you are not alone.

At one point in my life, I had a particular incident to happen to me that *totally* rocked my financial world—a situation that stopped me in my tracks and forced me to examine how I managed my money. I'll be telling you more about this incident later on in the book, and once I do, you'll never forget it. Hopefully you will learn from it and never have to go through it yourself.

This incident led me to do something that I had
never bothered to do before: I had to evaluate my life
and conduct an inventory of the thoughts and philosophies upon which I had been basing my money
decisions. When I dared to do this, I discovered that
there was a direct link between the way I thought
about money and my less-than-favorable financial
position. My inability to retain wealth, I saw, was
locked up by my mentality, and when it came to accumulating, saving, managing, and investing money,
I was forced to admit that I was *completely* ignorant.
What a humbling experience!

Lodged deeply in the recesses of my mind were
some old thoughts and beliefs about money that I
held to be sacred. However, these sacred thoughts
and beliefs that I had held so closely and protected
so fiercely for so many years were the very ones that
were causing me to stay broke! As much of a part of
my life as they had been, I had to be willing to identify
and uproot those thoughts, which would free me to
establish new patterns of behavior that led to the total
transformation of my financial life and brought me to
where I am today: living a life of financial stability and
wealth building! Listen, if I did it, you can too! Here's
the secret: it's all about what I did to unlock my mind.

Throughout this book, I will share my experiences
– good, bad and ugly – and the process I used to unlock
my mind. You will see some of the lessons labeled as
"Mental Keys." Each time you see a Mental Key, pay
close attention. In fact, take out your highlighter and
shade them in so that you can come back to them, because these are thought processes that you can use to

unlock your beliefs about money, debt, saving, credit cards, and ultimately, the purpose for building wealth.

The stories that I tell in this book about my own financial journey are authentic, the lessons are practical, and the principles are life-changing. Their application is detailed with step-by-step instructions as I walk you through my 10-Step Redemption Plan. Here's a word of advice for those of you who like to wait until the "perfect time" comes to make changes to your finances: do not wait to get things "just right" before you begin implementing the principles that I teach into your life. Instead, start right now where you are, regardless of your checking account balance, amount of debt, income level, or educational background. Today is that "perfect time" you've been waiting for, and the time to start is NOW! This plan will prepare your mind for the journey that you will take as you seek to transform your financial situation and see a dramatic increase in your progress towards building wealth. If you will just trust me to lead you in implementing the principles that you read, and if you follow them diligently, I am convinced that you will see a turnaround in your finances. Not only that, but both you and others close to you will see substantial changes in your life mentally and spiritually.

By the end of this book, you will be able to identify the enemies that attack your mind with unhealthy thoughts and philosophies about money and wealth, and you will understand what it takes to overcome the many obstacles that can block your financial progress.

At this point, you might be thinking, "I've read several financial books on the market that provide a system for budgeting and financial advice for saving money and building wealth, and they haven't worked for me so far. What makes this book so different?" That's a valid question. The good news is that I have a valid answer.

Unlock Your Mind...Unlock Your Money is unique because it delves into the root of things: it examines the very nature of *why* we manage our money the way we do. By dealing with issues like procrastination, planning, organization, and how they affect a person's money decisions, this book helps readers to address their habits and defeating thought patterns before it ever addresses their money. Further, the book provides a glimpse into how our money has our personality and how, as a result of this reality, our money usually behaves just like we do in other areas of our lives. While other books begin at teaching you how to handle your money, this book begins by first addressing your mentality. Once you get your money mind right, your money-handling habits will fall right into place!

Another thing that makes this book unique is that the principles discussed in it are largely built upon a sound biblical foundation. Thus, as you read through the chapters, you will see that there are several references to the Bible, which is the source of truth and wisdom that helps me to govern my life.

Remember, this book is titled *Unlock Your Mind... Unlock Your Money*, so keep an open mind as you read through it. Be intentional about absorbing the wisdom that I have learned through a combination of research and a series of *expensive* life lessons! Some of the information that you read will inevitably challenge your thinking and your relationship with money. When this happens, remind yourself that it has been designed to do just that. Instead of fighting it, go with it; accept the challenge. I am convinced that when you do, you will emerge on the other side victoriously waving the banner of financial freedom and living the life that others will only dream about!

Chapter One

IDENTIFY YOUR ENEMY

One of the most fearful mornings of my life happened when I was in elementary school. I woke up very afraid of what the day had in store for me. As I was getting dressed for school, I began to cry as thoughts of what would happen to me ran through my mind. I was terrified! I asked my mother if I could stay home for the day because "I wasn't feeling well." I tried to come up with any excuse to avoid getting on that school bus. However, nothing seemed to work. After several failed attempts to stay home, I reluctantly got on the bus to go to school.

As we approached the unloading area at my school, I looked out of the window and saw her standing there, waiting near the front door. I avoided eye contact with her hoping that she would not see me. I slipped into the building unnoticed and quietly sat down in the cafeteria to eat breakfast. However, the fear of what would soon happen had gripped me so tightly that I didn't have much of an appetite. In my mind, in my reality, I knew that the worst was about to happen in just a few minutes.

I began to sweat when the school bells sounded in the hallway, signaling that it was time to go to class. Today, the hallways seemed longer than ever. I felt like I had been walking forever as I slowly made my way from the cafeteria to my homeroom class. As I approached my classroom, I could hear her voice coming from inside the room, and instantly, my heart filled with fear; after all of my efforts to avoid her, the time had finally arrived—the moment at which I had to come face-to-face with her. I knew that regardless of what would happen next, I didn't stand a chance of getting out of this encounter. I was certain that the school principal and my mother were going to support her side of the story, and there was nothing that I could do about it.

As I entered the classroom and walked towards my seat, I saw her standing there looking very focused and intense. Before I could sit down, the door of the classroom slammed shut, and I instantly felt trapped! There was no escape! I knew that at this point, it would only be a matter of minutes before I would have to tell my teacher what had happened. What possible excuse would I be able to come up with to justify this?

Okay, I thought, *here she comes.* The closer she got to me, the faster and louder my heart beat, and I just *knew* that everyone around me could hear it. In an instant, my moment of truth was upon me, staring me in the face. At this point, I still had not come up with a good reason to justify my actions. The teacher continued to walk in my direction in what seemed like slow motion: seven students away, now five, now three. The suspense of what would happen when she reached my desk was too much; my little heart could hardly take it! How would she react when I told her?

At that moment, I experienced all of the emotions that I would imagine a deer would feel when he finds himself standing on a dark country road, and out of the darkness appears a blinding light that instantly paralyzes him, stopping him in his tracks. A deer in such a situation would not know how to react, and in my situation, neither did I.

I wondered, *Should I run? If so, in which direction?* Thoughts of how to deal with the encounter flooded my mind: *I can see her, but does she see me? Maybe if I don't move, she will skip me. Yeah… that's what I'll do! I will sit completely still and stare at my impending doom!* Well, needless to say, you know what typically happens to Bambi in these situations.

Finally, as she stood directly in front of my desk, she asked the dreaded question: "Derrick, where is your assignment?"

"Hello? Earth to Derrick! Where is your spelling assignment, son?" Initially, I gave no response. Then, suddenly, out of nowhere, I uttered the most intelligent response that I could come up with at the time. "Huh?" I answered.

"Your homework, son," she replied.

"Ughhh… I didn't do it, Ms. Bell."

With that, bracing for the unknown, I prepared for the worst. You see, I was the student who always had my assignments done. Up until now, I had never missed an assignment, and I was a "Straight A" student. Prior to this day, I had not even considered what the potential consequences would be for not completing my assignment. Would I be suspended from school or receive a paddling? Back then, in the early 90's, teachers were still allowed to paddle students, so I just knew I had one coming!

This was the moment of truth – so what would it be? Ms. Bell simply replied, "Okay. Just turn it in tomorrow."

WHAT?! I mean *really*? That was it? No suspension, paddling or anything else that I had dreamt up as a potential consequence for myself?
"Am I going to get in trouble, Ms. Bell?" I asked.
"No, just turn it in tomorrow," she answered.

Wow! I simply could not *believe* that I had been living in such tremendous fear since I had awakened that morning, only to now find out that there would be no consequence for not doing my assignment! Now, I was relieved... but I was also confused at the same time. Up to this point in my life, the rules were to prioritize the things that I <u>had</u> to do, and then I could do the things that I <u>wanted</u> to do. As I sat there at my desk trying to process this re-writing of "the rules" that I had just experienced, I reached a conclusion: "I guess," I muttered silently to myself, "being disciplined and prioritizing the things I 'needed' to do first were not as important as I thought."

I can't remember anything that I learned from the curriculum in school that day or during that year for that matter. However, I clearly remember the unforgettable life lesson that I learned that day. Today, I now realize that this experience as a fifth grader actually set the foundation for how I functioned in life for many years to come. The lesson that I learned that day was this: if I did not do the things that I needed to do in a timely manner, there would be no *immediate* consequences. Surely, communicating such a lesson was not the intent of my teacher, and I'm sure that it could not be found on her lesson plans for the day. However, in my young mind, that was my interpretation of the event that had taken place.

> *Procrastination was the first enemy that I identified as a mental foe that hindered my progress.*

That day, that one critical, unforgettable and defining moment that I experienced in the fifth grade gave birth to one of the most formidable enemies in my life. Even as an adult, I still have to fight and contend with the influence of this opponent on a daily basis. What I encountered that day was the formal introduction to procrastination. Later in life, procrastination was the first enemy that I identified as a mental foe that hindered my progress. This leads us to our first mental key.

Mental Key #1: THE ENEMY IS IN YOUR MIND!

In my experience, I've accepted the fact that procrastination is possibly the biggest mental enemy that we have to contend with when it comes to completing tasks, executing visions and reaching our goals. Procrastination always seems to convince us to believe that we will have more time, at a later time, just in the nick of time, to get things done.

The persuasive enemy that it is, procrastination causes us to delay things of importance, and oftentimes it will convince us to prioritize doing things that provide immediate gratification over things for which we must wait to experience a reward. For example, if you had a choice to either go and do something fun with your friends or stay home and do homework, which would you _want_ to do?

It is right in the middle of making these decisions that procrastination is its most effective, because it will always convince you to delay what you _need_ to do in order to do what you _want to do._

So why do so many people procrastinate?

I believe that there are multiple reasons why people tend to procrastinate. Some people are just flat out lazy! They lack the drive to do anything productive because it takes too much effort on their part. Others lack discipline. Those who lack discipline have a dif-

12

ficult time staying committed to anything for sustained periods of time. Let's not forget about the group that is excuse-driven, meaning something or someone else is always the reason that they cannot complete their task. Perhaps some people may procrastinate simply because they lack the knowledge that they need to complete their assignment, task, or goal.

In either case, if you look just beneath the obvious reason for procrastinating, fear is almost always in the corner whispering sweet nothings of doubt and telling you all the reasons that you should delay doing what you need to do. I'm reminded of an image I once saw on television. There was a man who was at the brink of making a critical decision, and standing on his shoulders were two little men; one representing good, and the other representing evil. In one ear, the man is hearing faith saying, "Go for it! You can do this!" and in the other ear, he hears the voice of fear saying, "You know this is not going to work, right?" More often than not, fear emerges as the victorious winner.

I believe that fear is one of the primary reasons that people tend to procrastinate. Such anxiety could be based largely on a fear of failing or being viewed by others as a failure. Without doubt, failing is one of the greatest fears of many people. No one wants to be perceived as someone who set out to do something and it didn't work. Consequently, many will settle for doing nothing instead of doing something and potentially failing at it. These individuals are usually satisfied with merely fantasizing about success in lieu of actually pursuing it. Engaging in a dialogue with others about what they "should have", "would have" and "could have" done or what they "will do some day" is good enough for them.

There are also those who procrastinate because they are perfectionists. If these guys lack sufficient details and information needed to ensure the project is "perfect", they will delay working on it altogether. This is oftentimes referred to as engaging in the "paralysis of analysis". The paralysis of analysis simply means becoming stuck and action-less due to their over-analysis of information in hopes of eliminating any potential of failure. Consequently, the task is usually never completed on time, and more often than not, the task becomes completely abandoned or aborted altogether.

Take a moment to think about which (if any) of these procrastination fears you have and how they may have impacted your life. If you fall into any one of the fore-mentioned categories and are willing to admit that you have a problem with procrastination, you are already on the right track.

What is the cost of procrastination?

- Have you ever said any of the following?

- Someday I'll start exercising.

- Someday I'll start saving money.

- Someday I'll start eating right.

- Someday I'll go and visit my family members.

- Someday I'll get right with God.

These are some of the most costly areas in which people commonly procrastinate. All of these actions are vitally important for a holistic and productive life. However, despite their level of importance, because of procrastination, we put them off for a later date or a more convenient time, delaying the very things that will help us live the kind of life that we dream of daily.

> *There are clearly negative consequences associated with delaying action in each of these important areas of our lives.*

There are clearly negative consequences associated with delaying action in each of these important areas of our lives. For example, the longer you put off exercising, the faster your health will deteriorate. Your quality of life will diminish at a much faster rate than those who have a routine exercise regimen. Proper diet and exercise are proven to enhance the quality of one's physical life while simultaneously reducing the risk of diabetes, obesity, heart problems, and other illnesses related to unhealthy eating practices and sedentary lifestyles.

The same negative consequences apply when it comes to delaying action in your finances. The longer you put off saving money, the longer you will be forced to work in order to maintain your lifestyle as you reach retirement age. Also, without having money in savings, you will always be at risk of being dependent upon creditors and family members to assist you when circumstances of life present you with emergencies that will require immediate access to money. Furthermore, you will not be able to enjoy the feeling of security that having a savings provides in unstable economic times. Procrastination when it comes to your family has its own unique set of consequences. The longer you put off spending time with your loved ones, the fewer memories you will have with them. When they pass away—and everyone will one day—you will regret not spending more quality time with them. Because death is permanent, you will never have an opportunity to make up for lost time with loved ones once they are gone.

Then, there are consequences that many of us are intimately familiar with when it comes to credit. The longer you put off paying your bills on time, the more money you will waste on paying late fees. Ultimately, your credit score will be negatively affected, and this will cost you more money in the long run. In the eyes of lenders, you will be viewed as "high risk," and you will be penalized for it by paying substantially higher interest and fees. Even essential services like water and electricity will require you to put down a security deposit before they will provide services to you as a result of your history with paying your bills late.

Perhaps one of the *most important* areas in which people delay action is that of developing a relationship with God. The longer you put off establishing a relationship with God through His Son Jesus Christ as your personal Lord and Savior, the more you gamble with your eternal destination. Not only do you gamble with eternity, but you will also miss out on the fulfillment of living a life pleasing to God now. There is such a joy and peace that comes with living a God-centered life. I personally wish everyone could experience the satisfaction and comfort of knowing that the eternal God is pleased with them based on the works that Christ fulfilled on the cross. However, God will never force anyone to accept His invitation to have a relationship with Him. This is a free will decision that each individual will have to make on his own. By declining the invitation to have a relationship with God, you will be subject to eternal separation from His presence in eternity, and since we do not know when our last day on earth will be, if we are wise, we will not delay action; we will accept His invitation now!

In virtually any situation, there will be a high cost for procrastination. If we were to ever compare where we are in life with where we think we should be by now, I'm willing to bet that procrastination reared its ugly head at some point and convinced us to put off our important tasks until later. Later eventually became one day, one day became someday, and you have been residing on "someday isle" ever since.

So if I've identified potential reasons why I procrastinate and the cost of procrastination, how do I overcome procrastination?

There are several keys to overcoming procrastination. I will provide for you four short but powerful steps to eliminate this debilitating habit. However, understand that each one requires you to make a shift in your thinking!

17

Step 1: Prioritize your time

The first key to overcoming procrastination is to prioritize your time. Time management is critical to preventing procrastination. If you set a definite deadline by which your important tasks need to be completed and focus solely on meeting that deadline, you will instantly limit the various opportunities that will arise for the purpose of distracting you and throwing you off task.

Step 2: Plan your day ahead of time

Start your day off with the things that you *must* get done that day; set everything else aside and begin working on these things immediately. By doing this, you will realize that there are a lot more hours in your day, week and month! By pre-planning your day, you mentally allow your mind to think about the things you will need to accomplish ahead of time, and therefore you will eliminate the potential for time-killers to interrupt your day.

Step 3: Establish a cadence

A cadence is a military term that is normally used in a song format. It creates a tempo or rhythm that everyone involved can identify with and set their pace to, and it is usually used when soldiers are marching in formation to keep them in stride, moving as one unit. A cadence is systematic, and it creates consistency to such a degree that the outcome becomes predictable. The cadence establishes the pattern by which everything and everyone else is governed. By establishing a cadence, you can reduce the potential for procrastination. You will easily be able to tell when you're "off-beat," or not in cadence with your schedule.

Step 4: Accept 100% responsibility

By accepting full responsibility for the expected outcome, you will significantly reduce the potential for procrastination because you remove the ability to blame someone else for the results or lack thereof. As long as someone else can be held equally responsible for completing the assignment, you will subconsciously use this as an escape route to avoid being accountable. When you accept full responsibility, you are agreeing to see the project through to completion, and you are saying, "I'm responsible for the outcome —good or bad."

Thus, overcoming procrastination takes:

- Prioritizing your time

- Planning your day ahead of time

- Establishing a cadence

- Accepting 100% responsibility

Initially, these steps will likely be difficult. In order to make the transition a little easier, allow for a little "fun time" in your list of things to do. Just make sure that the fun time is contingent upon the completion of your priority items and that it appears at the bottom of the list, not the top! This will accomplish a dual purpose: it serves as a type of reward system while keeping you motivated to plow through the list of all of the things that you need to do. There's no harm in rewarding yourself for accomplishing your goals with a little fun!

When it comes to accomplishing your wealth building goals, here's a simple formula to remember: 1) Set a goal 2) Accomplish the goal 3) Reward yourself 4) Repeat steps as needed.

Chapter Two

HOUSTON, I HAVE A PROBLEM!

Fast forward 20 years from my 5th grade experience. I was now living in Houston, Texas and had become a successful real estate agent. I'd built a good reputation for myself and had also acquired an impressive list of wealthy real estate investors.

My primary marketing strategy was to find profitable investment deals and present them to investors who were buying rental income property in Texas. I, myself, owned two multi-family rental properties at the time with a total of six rental units, so working with other investors was perfect on-the-job training for me. In fact, I was able to learn a lot from their experiences when they acquired new property. I then applied what I had learned to my own acquisitions. I learned how to manage multiple properties that the investors acquired without personally being exposed to any liability or risk. Therefore, whenever I wanted to acquire more property for myself, I was able to avoid costly mistakes that many new investors usually make.

Unlike my clients, I did not have any wealth. However, I did have good credit and a desire to make some quick money in the real estate market. I'd read several books on how to get rich utilizing real estate. I was convinced that it was easy, since everyone else was telling me how much money they "could" make by simply buying property with "OPM": Other People's Money.

Before I go on with my story, I have a confession to make. Like many others, I became a victim of the late night infomercials that promised instant success and prosperity in real estate with the simple purchase of a "no money down" real estate investing CD or system. I know you've seen them. In fact, I'm willing to bet that you probably have one in your closet collecting dust right now! If so, leave it there. Why? Very few people have actually become wealthy from "no money down" real estate purchases. There are a lot of hidden factors that are not explained in the selling of those products that are required for you to become a profitable real estate investor.

If you do not have the knowledge and the resources to acquire, manage and sustain the properties that you purchase, you will only create a stressful job for yourself that will ultimately become a nightmare. This will make more sense as you continue to read through the book.

THE GREAT REAL ESTATE COMMISSION

In October of 2007, one particular investor called me looking for a deal of 10 to 15 rental units. Wow! This was a big deal for me! I would usually work with individuals purchasing only one or two units at a time. With this deal, I felt that I had made it to the big leagues at last, and it was *finally* my turn at bat! In fact, as I hung up the phone with the investor, the theme song "Moving On Up" from the television show *The Jeffersons* came to mind, and I began to happily sing along. I was about to get my piece of the pie!

The investor had told me exactly what he was looking for, and I immediately found the perfect deal for him. The package deal for the investment units came to a little over $1.2 million. My fee for brokering the deal was 3% of the sales price, which would equate to more than $36,000 in commission for me. Such a commission in one year is not a lot of money in the real estate business, but $36,000 in one paycheck is something to get excited about!

Being a little country boy from Lake Providence, Louisiana, I thought that once I'd received this commission, I would be rich! Well, okay... I knew I wouldn't *literally* be rich, but for me, it would be the closest thing to being rich that *I'd* ever experienced! In fact, most of the people in my family didn't even make $36,000 in an entire year!

I was neither accustomed to nor prepared to receive that type of money. I thought, *What am I going to do with "all" of this money?*

The closing on that real estate deal took place the first week of February, 2008. WOW! This was the biggest check I'd ever held in my hands, and it was all mine to do with it whatever I wished. I was a thousand-aire!

Like most people who are not accustomed to having large sums of money at one time, I did not have the faintest clue of how to handle my big payday. Mind you, I was not *totally* reckless with it—well, not in my mind, at least. I say that because although I grew up poor, I never fully adopted the concept of "poverty spending" or "conspicuous consumption," often characterized by someone buying things like a $1,500 car and spending $5,000 on a paint job, sound system, and rims. I didn't stand in line for hours to pay $500 for the new Air Jordan athletic shoes. However, while I prided myself on not spending my money on these things, what I *did* spend my money on was just as stupid!

You see, just one month after receiving my biggest commission ever, around the middle of March of 2008, I had *no idea* where the majority of that money was. I did, however, know where it *wasn't*: in my bank account! I had consumed over $36,000 in less than a month. Unbelievable!

I know what you're thinking: *You did what?* Yes, you read it right. More than $36,000 in one month! The worst part about it all is that I didn't take a luxury vacation or buy any furniture, cars, boats, jewelry, etc., so I didn't even have much of anything to show for it. Yes, I'll admit, I was living the good life for approximately one month. As a matter of fact, I was literally "balling out of control" with all of my newfound "wealth." However, when it was all said and done, I still had the majority of the same debts and bills as I did the month before. Nothing had changed once my "money high" wore off. Financially, I was still in the exact same place as I was prior to receiving the commission...BROKE! Ouch! What a painful reality.

MENTAL KEY #2: LEARN FROM THE MISTAKES OF OTHERS

Charlie Love (my father) once gave me a profound piece of advice. He said "Son, you won't live long enough to make all of the mistakes in the world, so at some point you have to learn from others what not to do." I'd always wondered how people who won millions of dollars from the lottery could be broke after only a short period of time. I even remember criticizing athletes and entertainers who'd made millions of dollars in their careers but were once again broke after only a few years. Now that I had been given my own little "lottery experience," I saw just how easy it was to blow through large sums of money when you didn't have a proper plan and the right mentality to handle the money.

Quick question: If you received a large amount of money (over $50,000) unexpectedly, would you know what to do with it to make it grow and work for you right now? How long do you think you could hold on to it?

After coming to the realization that we were once again broke, my wife and I had an emergency, mandatory, "Come to Jesus" meeting (a moment of transparent, honest confession for our sins) to discuss this rude awakening—the realization that "all" of the money was gone.

- *Who* got "all" of our money?

- *What* did we spend "all" of the money on?

- *When* did we spend "all" of the money?

- *Where* did "all" of the money go?

- *Why* did we spend "all" of the money?

Maybe you've never had a "Come to Jesus" meeting with your spouse, but that particular night, there were things said that were *not* on the God-approved communication list!

Much to our dismay, we quickly discovered that we hadn't been robbed by masked gunmen. No one wrote any checks without our knowledge. There was no emergency surgery required for anyone. There were no major vehicle repairs done, nor renovations to the house. We had just simply blown through over $36,000 and we couldn't figure out where the money went. I did, however, know that a large portion, approximately $7,200 went to my church in the form of tithe and offerings (ten percent to tithe and at least ten percent to offerings), but outside of this, we were absolutely clueless about the rest of the money.

MENTAL KEY #3: BE WILLING TO THROW OUT OLD THINKING

I left the meeting with two realizations. My first realization was that whatever I thought I knew about money, I wanted to *unlearn—fast!* My old way of thinking about money had to go, because it was doing nothing but leading me straight to the poor house! My money management skills were obviously not working very well. No one had ever really taught me about money, and this experience made that painfully obvious.

The second realization was that once I got rid of my old money mindset, I needed to fill that void with new information about money. I needed to learn how to manage my money the way that the wealthy manage their money. I realized that every dollar that came through my hands needed to have a **purpose** and an **assignment** in order for it to be productive. Prior to this moment, my money operated like a wild, untamed horse. It simply ran free without any sense of purpose, control or direction. My money had become so out of control by now that trying to tame it at this point seemed completely hopeless. After this sobering financial fiasco, I began to do some research on how money should be handled and how it really works. In doing so, I did not request the opinions of other broke people (i.e., my opinionated friends, family members, co-workers, etc.). I did not solicit advice from people who had a lot of material things but no wealth. You know who these people are: the ones that wear their wealth on their backs with expensive name-brand clothing and jewelry from high-profile designers, that carry their wealth around on their handbags and showcase it in their homes, or that drive their wealth by investing substantial amounts of money into expensive cars in order to "look the part" and portray an image of success. No, this group of people had supplied me with the information I currently had concerning managing money. They were the source of my old information, and my old information was getting me nowhere.

There's a saying in Texas that describes these types of people. We refer to them as having "All hat and no cattle." In essence, they are full of big talk, pretending to be something that they are not, but they have no substance to back up their status.

In my quest to learn about money, I wanted to talk to wealthy people. No, not the "Wannabes," or the "Gonnabes" but the real, practical, and under-the-radar wealthy people. You know, the wealthy people that look like the everyday Joe; the ones who live next door and who do not attempt to impress others with lavish displays of their wealth. The types of wealthy people that were not flashy, that lived in modest homes, and that drove quality used vehicles for which they paid cash.

I wanted to talk to business owners who had built a successful business from the ground, and entrepreneurs who had taken an idea and turned it into a tangible product or service that produced substantial amounts of income. I was looking for someone who earned less than $100k a year but still managed to have a net worth of over $1 million in assets. I wanted to learn the financial disciplines that the wealthy practiced as a lifestyle so that I, too, could become one of them. This newfound insight would be the source that would put me on the correct path to wealth building.

> *There is one who pretends to be rich, but has nothing; another pretends to be poor, but has great wealth.*
> **Proverbs 13:7**

My research taught me a lesson about the wealthy that was particularly enlightening: the people with the *real* wealth were not easily noticeable based upon their accumulation of flashy material goods. Just because people have nice looking things does not mean that they have any wealth. I can attest to this myself, because while I definitely had stuff, I did *not* have any wealth! At the conclusion of my research, I realized there were a lot of thoughts and philosophies that I had to delete from my mind's money files in order to make room for and save this new-found information. This was a mandatory exercise if I was going to change my financial future.

Words of Wisdom: Proverbs 13:7—*There is one who pretends to be rich, but has nothing; another pretends to be poor, but has great wealth.*

MENTAL KEY #4: IF YOU'RE FAT, SAY "I'M FAT!" DON'T LIE TO YOURSELF!

I remember a specific incident when my wife and I had just moved to Houston, Texas. We were still fairly young in our marriage at the time, so I was very much still in the "impress my woman" mode. My wife had a little Nissan Altima that her mother had financed for her. I hated that car, and I desperately wanted to "upgrade" my woman. However, I didn't have any money available. So I, being the big shot that I was, went to a luxury car dealership and "financed" for my wife a slightly used BMW.

I remember looking at my wife with this look of, "You see what kind of man you have, girl? I can have whatever I want, whenever I want it!" I felt this great deal of satisfaction because I could make such an acquisition for my wife. Silly me! That BMW added an additional $18,000 to my existing debt load, but I didn't care! Why? Because I was more impressed by other people's perception of us being this young successful couple living the dream. We had it going on—well, on the surface at least!

At the time, I was only 23-years-old, and I had accumulated nearly $300,000 in debt by way of real estate investments, credit cards, and automobiles. If I was lucky, at any given moment I might have had

$3,000 in savings. Hello! Take another look at those numbers. Those numbers suggest that I only had one percent of cash on hand to match my debt! I had built a house of cards, and little did I know, they would all come tumbling down soon.

Being overweight is easily noticed in our physical bodies because we, along with others, can see the excess fat that we've accumulated. When it comes to our physical bodies, we buy bigger clothing to mask the weight gain; ladies have become masterful at using undergarments like Spanx and girdles to "suck and tuck" in their excess weight in order to keep it out of view.

However, when it comes to our finances, it is much more difficult for us to see how fat we've become, and it is nearly impossible for others to see the weight that we've gained, because most of us keep our true financial status covered up.

In either situation, when we have become overweight, we are in desperate need for someone to be brutally honest with us and tell us (in a caring and loving way) the truth: My friend, you are FAT! However, this is easier said than done. It can be a difficult task for someone (especially our loved ones) to tell us that we're fat, especially when most of our friends and family members understand the risk of becoming alienated if they tell us such a difficult-to-digest truth. We have built our lives and social circles around people that affirm us, and anything not affirming can easily become offensive to emotionally immature people. Most people will not risk their relationship with us by telling us the truth about ourselves. Consequently, we walk around obese and unhealthy while those around us look upon us with pity, never daring to confront us with the truth of our reality.

You can only live in denial for so long. Eventually, the excess weight will catch up with you and force you to address the issue. Physically, it can come in the form of diabetes, high blood pressure, high cholesterol, heart attacks, strokes, etc. Financially, it usually appears in the form of poor credit, foreclosures, repossessions, bankruptcy, judgments, etc.

After looking deep into my financial mirror, I finally saw the fat man that I had become. I could no longer hide or remain in denial. I realized that I had an unhealthy dependence on my credit. If I couldn't buy it, I borrowed to get it. When there was no cash available, I always had my little plastic "buy it now and pay for it later," card in my wallet. At the time, however, I was unconscious of the mounting debt that I was accumulating and the consequences that would follow.

Just as I had embarked on a journey to understand the proper methods of managing money effectively, my house of cards that I had been building with all of this debt was starting to crumble. I could hear cracking sounds underneath my feet. Imagine a stack of cards that someone had used to make a beautiful pyramid. At the base of the pyramid are the support cards that serve as the foundation upon which the rest of the cards stand. My dependence on credit was the foundation for the financial house of cards that I'd built. Now, imagine what happens when you start removing cards from the foundation. The outcome is clear. The entire stack of cards that once was a beautiful pyramid would come tumbling down. Well, that's exactly what happened to me! I had built a life on borrowed money, and now, it was slowly beginning to crumble.

The first sign that things were falling apart was that the first rental property that I'd purchased using OPM, other people's money began to show signs of trouble. I began having difficulties with keeping reliable tenants that paid their rent on time. As a result, I had to pay the mortgage out of my already overburdened income. Eventually, the burden of paying two mortgages became too difficult, and I consciously decided to allow the rental property to go into foreclosure. Of course, by now my credit that I had been so dependent upon was no longer available to me because of the foreclosure. Therefore, I was forced to use cash and save for the things I wanted. This leads me to my next mental key.

MENTAL KEY #5: CASH IS YOUR FRIEND. TAKE ADVANTAGE OF THE RELATIONSHIP!

At this point in my life, the concept of saving money in order to purchase things in cash was foreign and antiquated. I mean really... who *does* that? Without even realizing it, I had become a victim of the world's money management mentality which is characterized by the following: simply borrow money for the things that you can't afford to buy with cash! In our society of hyper consumption, borrowing money is simply a way of life.

Our current economy is built upon the concept of borrowing now and paying later. Carrying cash on you will cause people to look at you funny—as if *you're* the weird one! It has become urban legend that carrying cash will surely set you up to be robbed in a dark alley by street thugs who are equipped with infrared binoculars that can detect cash in your pockets. Truthfully, the odds of you *being* robbed by someone because you are carrying cash are much slimmer than the times you've *been* robbed by banks and credit card companies while using their plastic.

Speaking of cash, let me explain the benefits of using cash versus credit. Having cash is like having a master negotiator with you. When you are buying with cash money, you are likely to get a much better deal on your purchase.

For example, I recently purchased a used pickup truck. I purchased this truck for the sole purpose of hauling my boat whenever I had an opportunity to go fishing. I was looking for a used truck, so it didn't have to be pretty or fancy. I stumbled across a deal where a guy was selling his truck for $3,000. I did a little research on the truck, and the resale value of the truck in good condition was $4,500. When I went to test drive it, it met all of the pre-determined basic requirements that I had. Not wanting to do a lot of haggling back and forth on the price, I simply asked the gentleman, "What's the lowest amount of money you'll take for the truck?"

He replied, "I can't do any less than $2,800." *Note: I instantly saved $200 just by asking a simple question.* Without any further dialogue, I countered his offer with 15 crisp $100 bills, simply placing the stack of $100 bills in his hand and then waiting for his response. I didn't tell him how much money it was prior to giving it to him. I just let him *feel* the cash in his hands, and then he became *attached* to it and *protective* of it. After he counted the money, he smiled, hesitated for a moment, and then asked, "Whose name do you want on the title?" Sold!!!

In this example, if I would have tried to negotiate that much money off of the price and then attempted to get financing, the guy would have probably laughed at me and told me to get the hell off of his property! However, by having cash in hand, it communicated to the seller that I was serious and capable of making the purchase right then and there. That's the power of using cash over credit.

Using cash will make the transaction somewhat "emotionless." By that, I mean you will not be impressed by hearing the infamous "you're approved" which usually is the precursor to a financial catastrophe. Those words are like sweet music to the ears of those needing financing approval to purchase things. However, using cash allows your logic to have a greater chance of being heard over your emotions. Hey, if in the event that you don't get a good deal, take your cash to someone who *will* give you a great deal. As the old saying goes, "Cash is king"! The next time you make a large purchase, try using cash and a little negotiation and watch with amazement the great deal you get!

MENTAL KEY #6: STOP OVEREATING!

Just as many people overeat natural food, other people have a tendency to overeat when it comes to material consumption. I once was convinced that I could purchase whatever I wanted as long as I could "afford" the payments from my income. I've lived comfortably from check to check, and when I did so, I thought that this was normal. I was on a perpetual earn-to-consume treadmill, and I was running really fast. Remember the fat man that I told you I had become earlier? I got that way because I bit off more debt than I could chew by spending more than I earned.

My greed and desire to have things that I couldn't afford continued to add to my debt load, and it forced me to spend more and save less from my income. I had slowly become *financially obese*. All of my income was going to support my habit of accumulating more junk. However, instead of *losing* the junk in my trunk, I kept *adding* new junk to my trunk. I guess you could say I was a "consumer junkie."

Let's examine this earn-to-consume treadmill. Think about the design of a treadmill for a moment. When you exercise on a treadmill, you select and then respond to the tempo and the speed that YOU set on the machine. While the treadmill does not initiate your speed or tempo for you, it keeps you moving at the level at which you told it to operate. The higher you set your speed, the faster you must run in order to keep pace with the treadmill. If you get tired and fall behind in pace, it will forcefully throw you off of it.

This is the imagery that I want you to remember when you set the pace for your consumption habits. The more you consume, the more you will have to work in order to earn more income just to keep up. The more debt you consume, the faster you will have to run on the earn-to-consume treadmill in order to keep pace. On my journey to financial freedom, I soon discovered that I was not the only person dealing with this issue. I discovered that there were millions of people that have a membership at the same gym with me, and we were all running on the same type of earn-to-consume treadmill. Why do you think they use the phrase "Keeping up with the Joneses"? The Joneses are running too! The good thing is that there is no long-term contract to this gym, and you can cancel your membership at any time!

You may have already identified some areas where your cravings for unhealthy things may have caused you to gain a few extra pounds of financial fat. By the time you finish this book, you will be able to look into your own financial mirror and see where you may have picked up a few extra pounds. However, you will also be equipped to trim those pounds of financial fat if you utilize the mental keys provided and the 10-Step Redemption Plan discussed later in the book.

Chapter Three

LAYING THE RIGHT FOUNDATION

Having a solid foundation or starting point is necessary for the completion of any endeavor. Whether you're starting a business, building a home, or preparing for marriage, the right foundation is absolutely critical to its success.

As I mentioned earlier, I have years of experience with buying and selling real estate. I have learned from these experiences about how a home is built and about which critical elements are necessary to build a quality home. What I discovered was that the amount of time and quality invested in the foundation of the home would determine the overall quality of the home once it was completed. If the foundation was built with poor workmanship, the entire structure would be at risk of being destroyed. Consequently, everything built on the faulty foundation would ultimately be a waste of time and money because it would not last.

Therefore, as we walk together on this journey, I want to lay the proper foundation. There are several things that need to be established up front in order for you to have the proper mindset about money as you continue in this book.

> *"For he sees that even wise men die; the stupid and the senseless alike perish and leave their wealth to others."*
>
> **Psalm 49:10**

WHOSE MONEY IS IT ANYWAY?

Words of Wisdom: *Psalm 49:10 – "For he sees that even wise men die; the stupid and the senseless alike perish and leave their wealth to others."*

The Bible says in Psalm 50:10-12 that "the cattle on a thousand hills belong to God" and "the earth is the Lord's and the fullness thereof." The Bible also says that all silver and gold belongs to God in Haggai 2:8. Ultimately, if we agree that the Bible is true and that God is the Creator of the earth, then it stands to reason that we would agree that the contents of the earth also belong to Him. Thus, all of the resources to which we have access—including our money—originate from God and consequently belong to God.

Not only does wealth originate from God, but in the end, the money that we have will all go back to Him. If you don't believe this, just take a quick look back at history. You'll see that everyone, from the world's richest people to the poorest of men left their wealth behind when they died. Even the Egyptian pharaohs who attempted to be buried with their treasures realized when they arrived at their final destination that their treasures did not make the transition with them. Further, since we all personally know of someone who has died in our lifetime, we are certain of the reality of death. We can personally testify to the fact that their treasures did not travel with them. Instead, these things were left behind for others to utilize and reap the benefits from until they themselves would have to make their final appointment to check out. The principle of the last man standing applies here, and according to the Bible, God Himself will be the last man standing (figuratively speaking).

GOD MADE US STEWARDS

In order to have the proper perspective about money, we must recognize that we are not owners of our money, only stewards. According to the Bible, a steward is one who manages the resources and affairs of another. A steward has parameters and limitations on what he can and cannot do with the owner's property and resources.

To better help you understand the concept of a steward, allow me to attempt to provide a comparison for you to reference. In a lot of ways, a steward is like a real estate property manager, for they share similar responsibilities and functions.

As a realtor, I started my career managing properties for out-of-state investors. As the property manager, I had limited authority. I would approve or deny an applicant that wanted to lease a property based on my subjectivity. I would also collect the revenues/rent for the month on behalf of the owner. In most cases, the tenants never actually spoke to the true owners; instead, they had to bring their issues and concerns to me. I would then take care of the issue based upon my delegated authority. As far as that property was concerned, I was the representative who spoke on behalf of the owner.

I understood my role as a manager, though. For example, I could not independently decide to sell the property. I could not take out a loan against the property. I could not collect the rents and spend the money. It was not my property to take ownership of; I simply managed the resources and the affairs of the property for the owner.

The industry standard that a property manager will charge an owner to manage his property is 10% of the owner's gross earnings. For example, if I managed a small apartment complex for someone and the gross rental income for the complex was $10,000 a month, I would receive $1,000 for my management fee. Isn't it interesting how property managers charge 10% to manage a residential property for others, and God requires believers to bring 10% of their gross earnings into His storehouse (your local church) in the form of the tithe? Is this a coincidence? Perhaps! You decide.

A hypothetical question:

What if God only allowed us to keep 10% of the income from the resources that we manage for Him, and we had to bring Him the other 90%? Many people complain about

*bringing back 10%, but in all actuality, we should be grate-
ful for being allowed to keep 90% and bring 10% back to
God. Let that marinate!*

MENTAL KEY #7: CHANGE YOUR PERSPECTIVE!

As it relates to our wealth and material possessions,
we must begin to see ourselves as property managers
for God. The money we have, the jobs, homes, cars,
children, etc., all belong to God. We can't take any of
these things away from this earth when we die. Therefore, since we cannot take them with us, we are simply
managing those things to which God has graciously
allowed us to have access while we are yet alive.

Like a property manager, if you are not managing
the resources and affairs correctly, you can be termi-
nated; the true owner will then find someone else to
manage his resources and affairs.

WHAT'S IN YOUR HANDS?

There is a great model in the Bible of what God
expects from us when it comes to managing His resources. In Matthew 25:14-30, Jesus gives the parable
(*a natural example of a kingdom concept*) of the talents (*a
form of currency*). This parable was based on the common knowledge of investing, and Jesus expected the
people of the day to understand investments. Jesus
shows us in this parable how He responds to the ser-

vants who had been faithful stewards and to those who were unfaithful with what He had given them.

In this parable, three men were given a certain number of talents. Two of the three men took what they had been given and multiplied (invested) it. Thus, they did more with what they had access to than the third man. The third man took what was given to him and simply buried (saved) it. He never attempted to invest or generate a return with it. Consequently, when the owner returned to the men looking for a return on his investment, the first two presented him with more than he gave them in the beginning. These two men were rewarded and praised, and ultimately, they were given more talents because they knew how to invest. However the third man, the one who buried his talent, only brought back what he was given. The owner was furious with this man, for he never even attempted to increase what he was given. Therefore, the owner condemned him, calling him wicked and lazy! What an indictment!

What have you done with the talents that God has entrusted you with in your lifetime? *Note that in this context, "talents" is referring to money, not your skills or abilities to sing, dance, shoot basketball, etc.* God expects us to be productive with the resources that He gives us to manage. Have you simply buried your talents somewhere that does not produce an increase, or have you been faithful over His resources and brought Him a return?

GOD... YOUR SILENT INVESTMENT PARTNER

In the book of Deuteronomy 8:18, God proclaims that it is He who gives us the ability or the power to get wealth. In other words, our life, health, strength, breath, and abilities all originated from God. God is the ultimate investment partner. He provides the "start-up capital" or "seed money" for us to grow and develop the resources that allow us to build wealth.

For example, the farmer didn't create the land in which he sows his seeds. God created that land. God also provided the seed that the farmer sows. The farmer simply uses what God created to produce a crop which in return yields a product that the farmer can sell to earn a living and build wealth. The oceans that contain the fish we eat were not created by man. God created the oceans and stocked them with fish, and the fishermen simply learned how to catch the fish and bring them to the marketplace. The foods that we eat did not originate with the chef who prepared them for us. God made the cow that the butcher cut into steaks for the chef to prepare. God supplied the salmon that the fisherman caught with his nets that was ultimately prepared by the chef and served in a restaurant to the customer. The chef simply prepared something that had already been created. In both of these examples, we see that multiple people were allowed to generate wealth based on what God had already created. The list could go on and on. Simply put, it is God who gives us the power or ability to generate wealth based on the resources that He has provided for us.

Chapter Four

TWO CULTURES IN CONTRAST

Words of Wisdom: 1 Corinthians 3:19 –
"For the wisdom of this world is foolishness
with God."

Does the philosophy or set of values and principles that you use to govern your finances really matter to you? If not, it should! After all, how do you know that what you are using to govern your finances is based on sound proven methods? The reality is that there are many aspects of our money mentality out of which we operate on a daily basis out of tradition, function, routine and culture.

We live in a world of contrasting philosophies and ideas: good vs. evil, Democrat vs. Republican, Baptist vs. Pentecostal, rich vs. poor, etc. However, the World's Economic Philosophies vs. God's Economic Principles might be the contrast that could make the biggest difference between your ability to achieve financial success or you maintaining your "broken budget" status quo. Each ideology will yield a different set of financial outcomes. Let's discuss some of the World's Economic Philosophies and see how they contrast with God's Economic Principles that are designed to lead you down the path to financial freedom.

World's Economic Philosophy #1: The key to building wealth is a High FICO/Credit Score!

When it comes to finances on an individual level, the world's economic philosophy advises you to build your credit score. Your credit score is a number generated by a computer program that takes all of your financial history into account and then produces a numerical figure that is designed to give the inquirer an idea of how well you manage your debts. You may have also heard it referred to as your "FICO score." The Fair Isaac Corporation (FICO) is a public company that provides analytics and decision-making solutions to lenders in order to assist them in determining if they will risk loaning money to an individual. Thus, your credit score is used primarily by lenders to determine if they are willing to "risk" loaning you money.

In my opinion, this credit scoring system was masterfully created as a tool to keep individuals dependent on using credit, and consequently, remaining in debt. Think about it. The only way to establish "credit" is to borrow money. Financial institutions, in exchange, will report monthly to the three major credit bureaus (Equifax, Transunion, and Experian) about whether you made your scheduled payments and whether they were on time. You can't have a favorable credit score without having some type of debt structure established in order to determine if you are creditworthy! Your credit score is determined by several factors. The two primary factors are the length of time that you've had the credit account (how long have you had this debt?) and the payment history (have you been paying your monthly payments on time?). The better your payment history and length of time with the debt looks, the better or higher your credit score will be.

The higher your credit score is (a 700 or higher score is typically considered high, or good), the easier it is for you to obtain a loan. The lower your credit score is (below 600 is typically considered low, or bad), the harder it is to get a loan. With a high credit score, you get favorable terms of repayment, which usually includes a lower interest rate on a loan. However, with a low credit score, you get the opposite, which is usually a much higher interest rate on the loan. This ultimately means that in the long run, it will cost more money out of your pocket to borrow the same amount of money as someone with a higher credit score.

I've fallen victim to the "credit score god" before. I'd become so committed to improving my credit score that, at the point I realized my score had dropped into the mid 600's, I went and got into more debt to "build" my score back into the 730 range. Remember, I relied heavily on my credit and loved hearing that spontaneous "You're approved!" when I applied for financing or loans.

Many financial advisors and economic professors preach the gospel of "building your credit" by going into debt. In essence, here is what they are saying:

borrow money to purchase something and be willing to pay the lender a profit (by way of interest accumulation) on the money you borrowed on a monthly basis. In exchange for the extra money you will give to them, they will report to the credit bureaus how excellent of a customer you are so that other lending institutions can now partake in taking your money at a high interest rate on a monthly basis.

God's Economic Principle #1
Rely on God's Favor
"A good name is to be chosen rather than great riches, loving favor rather than silver and gold."
Proverbs 22:1

When the Bible speaks about God's favor, it is referring to how He sees you. It means that God speaks favorably about you.

There are some people who can rely on their wealth to create opportunities for themselves that are usually reserved for the elect or the privileged class of society. Others rely on their families, fraternal or political connections to provide opportunities for themselves. However, for those of us who are not wealthy and who do not have a rich uncle to rely on for these things, God assures us that His favor will open windows of opportunity for us that nothing in our natural lives suggest should be opened. I would rather have the favor of God on my side than a large bank account, political connection, or rich relative.

I realize that money can't solve all of life's problems. However, there are some instances in which simply having access to money will instantly solve your problem. For example, if your car transmission goes out, you don't need God to fix that. This doesn't require faith; it requires "Franklins." Having some money available in the bank is all you need to remedy this problem with your car.

However, there are other instances in which money is irrelevant because it cannot solve your problem. I've been in several situations where, regardless of how much money I had available at my disposal, money could not have gotten me through the situation.

I remember when I was the ripe old age of 27-years-old, and out of nowhere, I had a brain aneurysm. This aneurysm was preceded by constant headaches, which were extremely abnormal for me. I went to doctors on multiple occasions, and they simply diagnosed the frequent headaches as being stress-related. The doctors would ask questions like, "Are you having money problems?" *Uhh… yeah! Who isn't having money problems, dude?* But what does that have to do with all of these excruciating headaches? Ignorant of how to treat or properly diagnose what was causing the headaches, doctors simply blew my frequent headaches off as a byproduct of stress and prescribed over-the-counter pain medicine as needed. Well, sure enough they had misdiagnosed my symptoms, and it nearly cost me my life! One evening in October 2006, it happened. My wife and I had just eaten dinner at a restaurant, and just as soon as we made it home, I had a seizure and collapsed on the floor. I'd just had a brain aneurysm with no forewarning. Just like that, I should have died! If you're not aware of what an aneurysm is, it is when an internal blood vessel in your body, usually in your brain or your stomach, swells and ultimately bursts or ruptures. Most often, when aneurysms occur in the brain, they are extremely life-threatening, and the situation rarely turns out favorably. In fact, most people who suffer from a brain aneurysm die within minutes of the rupture, never even making it to the hospital. The survival rate for brain aneurysms is less than 10%. Of the 10% of people who actually survive an aneurysm, a large percentage of them never recover fully to their original state. Many survivors suffer from paralysis, permanent memory loss, or they are left in an unconscious state living on machines.

Well, the mere fact that you are reading this book is an indication that none of the statistics for brain aneurysm sufferers applies to me! I made a full, 100% recovery after about three weeks in the hospital. The only indication that I've suffered a brain aneurysm is the small scar on my head that was left from the incision made during my brain surgery. MY GOD IS AWESOME!

Now you see, in my situation, the amount of money that I had in my bank account was totally irrelevant (at least until that $155,000 medical bill arrived at my house). It was only God's favor that allowed me to survive that experience. Thank you Lord!

Surely, God has demonstrated unmerited (undeserved) favor towards you at some point in your life. Take a moment to reflect on the times in your life when if it had not been for God's favor, you would have been in a really bad situation, and your money would have been irrelevant to change the state of your condition.

Note: If you're not a current believer in God, you may have referred to this situation as luck, or good fortune.

WORLD'S ECONOMIC PHILOSOPHY #2: BORROW MONEY FROM OTHERS/USE OTHER PEOPLE'S MONEY (OPM)

It is the cultural norm in North America to borrow money now and promise to pay it back later. The concept of saving up and using our own money is as outdated as typewriters, audio cassettes and pagers.

Economists and professors alike teach that it is wiser to use borrowed money to acquire large items such as homes, invest in business ventures, etc. They claim that using OPM places significantly less risk on the individual. In my opinion, borrowing money places *greater* risk on the individual. Consider this: if you borrow OPM for a business and the business is not profitable (which statistically speaking is very likely to happen), you are now faced with two options:

Option #1: <u>Walk away</u>. You will be more willing to walk away from the venture with little guilt because you have very little, if any capital of your own invested. However, the consequences of you walking away and the business failing are not as easily escaped as it appears to be on the surface. You will still be responsible for the money that you borrowed to launch the business, the expenses that you incurred while trying to operate the business and a host of other costs that come with operating a business.

Because you walked away, now your credit that you worked so hard to build will be damaged, if not ruined. The entity from which you borrowed the money will not simply say, "*You gave it your best shot! Therefore, we forgive the debt that you owe us because you tried.*" Instead, you will still be liable for repaying the loan. Any outstanding bills that you have with vendors, service providers, etc., will still be your responsibility. Creditors and collection agencies will pursue you relentlessly trying to collect the money you owe their clients. In the end, you will be spending your money one way or the other.

There's nothing like having to pay out new money earned today for old bills and expenses of yesterday that provide no current benefit to you. It's like paying for a wedding from a marriage that's already been dissolved; you're now divorced, but every month, you're reminded of the past failures of the marriage because you're still paying for the wedding reception, the ring, the cake, and the DJ (as a result of paying for the wedding with a credit card or loan).

Option #2: <u>File bankruptcy</u>. As an alternative to walking away, you could opt to file for some sort of bankruptcy or restructuring, which will cause an enormous amount of stress and headaches, not to mention the fact that bankruptcy will literally destroy your credit. Further, depending on the strength of your marriage (if applicable), you could possibly be facing a divorce due to the financial strain that the marriage is now under (one of the leading causes of divorce for most couples is money problems).

How many times have you seen these risk factors advertised by a bank or credit card company that was trying to sell you their primary product: debt? NEVER!

Note: Loaning consumers money is how banks make their money and stay profitable. Banks are not "non-profit organizations." Their sole purpose for being in business is to make a profit off of you, the consumer. You do realize that debt is a product sold to us by banks and credit card companies, right? Think about it. When you go to retail stores, they sell tangible products. Well, the banks sell debt as a product.

GOD'S ECONOMIC PRINCIPLE #2: BORROWING CREATES INSTANT BONDAGE

"THE RICH RULE OVER THE POOR AND THE BORROWER IS SLAVE TO THE LENDER."
PROVERBS 22:7

In Deuteronomy 15:6, the Bible addresses in-depth how God feels about believers borrowing money. In this passage of scripture, God is dealing with Israel concerning money management, giving, dealing with debts, etc. In this particular verse, God gives a direct order and a promise to His people. It states, "*For the*

Lord your God will bless you just as He promised you: you **shall lend** *to many nations, but you* **shall not borrow***; you shall reign over many nations, but they shall not reign over you."*

There is little room for interpretation when the word "shall" is used. Shall clearly does not mean something that's to be considered, contemplated, processed for clarity, etc. Instead, it means what it means: that this is something that WILL happen!

In addition, God also addresses how our attitude should be if we as believers have received a loan for someone or helped to secure a loan on someone else's behalf, better known as "co-signing." Proverbs 6:1-5 states, *"My son, if you become surety for your friend, if you have shaken hands in pledge for a stranger, you are snared by the words of your mouth; you are taken by the words of your mouth. So do this, my son, and deliver yourself; plead with your friend: Go and humble yourself; Give no sleep to your eyes, nor slumber to your eyelids. Deliver yourself like a gazelle from the hand of the hunter, and like a bird from the hand of the fowler.*

This passage of scripture shows us how God feels about believers owing someone. Although it does not specifically address the individual obtaining a loan, it clearly shows His disdain for others co-signing for a loan for someone else. Notice the word choice in this passage: *"Give no sleep to your eyes"* (don't go to sleep until this is resolved), *"Deliver yourself like a gazelle from the hand of the hunter"* (the hunter is usually a hungry lion and the gazelle is an animal similar to a deer). It's pretty clear that He didn't want us to be in this type of situation long. This type of language suggests only one thing: act immediately and run for your life! Runnnn!

Many believers may have already obtained a loan, co-signed for a friend or family member on a loan, or already have debt prior to coming to know God. That's why He provides a solution in the same sentence to those that have already become trapped in this situation. God ALWAYS provides a way out for His people!

Many believers who are new to the faith or those that are "seasoned" in the faith but have never had anyone address the financial teachings of God outside of lessons about the tithe and offerings may already be in bondage. This is why God deemed the topic of finances important enough to include in the scriptures. We see throughout the Bible how God always provides an opportunity for His people to be released from bondage. God, being the loving Father that He is, never wants to see His children in bondage to anyone or anything. The Bible makes this clear all throughout the scriptures.

WORLD'S ECONOMIC PHILOSOPHY #3: ACCUMULATE TREASURES ON EARTH

We all like to have nice things, and there's nothing wrong with desiring to have nice things in life. However, many people seem to be convinced that they can accumulate enough money and material possessions to "live their best life now." Therefore, many attempt to amass great wealth on earth, forgetting in the process of doing so that this is only a temporary stay. As we discussed earlier, none of the things that we accumulate on earth transfer over to our final destination after we die.

We are constantly sold on the idea of having all that we want in life *right now*. I believe that this is the primary reason that so many people are buried deeply in debt. We are overtaken by our emotions to get anything and everything that we want right now. If we see it, we feel like we deserve to have it; at least, this is what we tell ourselves. I've heard one time too many when someone says, "You work all of your life, so you should be able to get the things that you want. After all, that *is* why you go to work every day!" Unfortunately, this is the mentality of the poverty-stricken people of the world. While people who spend all they get because they "worked for it" fall on one end of the spectrum, the other extreme includes people who feel like they are building an empire of money and possessions so that they will never need to depend upon God or anyone else for their needs. Jesus would ask this person, *"For what profit is it to a man if he gains the whole world, and loses his own soul?"* Matthew 16:26

GOD'S ECONOMIC PRINCIPLE #3:
STORE YOUR TREASURES IN HEAVEN, NOT ON EARTH -
"DO NOT LAY UP FOR YOURSELVES TREASURES ON EARTH, WHERE MOTH AND RUST DESTROY AND WHERE THIEVES BREAK IN AND STEAL; BUT

LAY UP FOR YOURSELVES TREASURES IN HEAVEN, WHERE NEITHER MOTH NOR RUST DESTROYS AND WHERE THIEVES DO NOT BREAK IN AND STEAL. FOR WHERE YOUR TREASURE IS, THERE YOUR HEART WILL BE ALSO." MATTHEW 6:19

In this passage of scripture, Jesus is trying to help us understand the difference between temporary things and eternal things. I remember growing up and seeing moth balls in my grandmother's closet. I didn't know what they were for at the time, but I knew that they had a distinctive smell. I later learned that the moth balls were to prevent moths from eating holes in her clothing that had been stored away in her closet. Apparently, there was something in the scent of the moth balls that kept the moths away from her clothes.

Likewise, rust begins to accumulate when something is sitting for long periods of time with no activity or movement. Over time, the item is no longer good for use because it becomes corroded by the rust, and it loses its worth or value.

Then, thieves are constantly looking for the next victim from which they can steal. In fact, some people have made it their career to take from others. The news is filled with stories about people breaking into homes, stealing someone's purse, car, money, etc. When we store up our wealth on earth, this natural wealth faces all three of the threats Jesus mentioned: destruction by moth or rust or being stolen by thieves. These are temporary, perishable things, so why concentrate on laying up such treasures on earth? Instead, focus your energies on laying up treasures in heaven where they will be imperishable and eternal. When we store our treasures in heaven, they are protected.

You may be asking, *"How do I store up treasures in heaven?* You store up treasures in heaven by giving sacrificial gifts to your local ministry to support God's work. Surely, we know that there's nothing that we can *literally* give to God, because everything already belongs to Him. However, God commands us to give what we would give directly to Him to the church— His storehouse. He expects believers to financially support and sustain the ministries to which they are assigned. In addition to sustaining the ministry itself, God also expects believers to support and sustain the leader of the ministry: the pastor. Your leader should not be worried with issues like providing for his family or keeping the utilities at the church from being shut off; these are not issues that he should be focused upon while he is doing the work of ministry. These are items that should be taken care of because the people that the leader serves are obedient in bringing their tithes and giving sacrificial offerings to sustain the work of ministry. When your leader is consumed with these kinds of issues, this limits the time that he or she has to study, prepare, and minister the Word of God to you.

Chapter Five

WHO IS RESPONSIBLE FOR MY FINANCIAL WELL-BEING?

"In order to move from where you are, you first have to deal with where you are."
—Dr. Dana Carson, MBA,
Financial Stewardship Expert

After my experience with wasting more than $36,000 in one month, my first inclination was to blame my wife for my shortcomings. Yep, just like Adam in the Garden of Eden, my excuse was that it was the fault of that woman that God gave to me. After all, it is human nature to seek someone else to blame for the things that we do wrong, right? I mean, what else would you expect from me? It's in my natural DNA! Way back in the Garden of Eden, Adam set the precedence when he blamed Eve for causing him to eat the fruit from the forbidden tree. God had told Adam directly not to eat of the fruit, but Adam allowed the woman that God had created for him to influence him to go against what God said; and he ate the fruit anyway. It's in our nature to want to avoid taking personal responsibility for our actions, just like Adam.

MENTAL KEY #8: STOP LOOKING FOR SOMEONE TO BLAME!

At some point, when you take a good hard look at your financial condition, you will instantly begin trying to figure out how you got there and who is responsible. However, let's first begin by identifying who's **not** responsible for your financial failures.

The Government – Many people feel that the government is the reason that they are not prospering. These same people also tend to blame the President for their financial hardships. Targeting the President or a government official as the cause of why our finances are the way they are is simply to use them as an easy target; it allows us to divert attention away from our own responsibility (or lack thereof) in causing our financial condition.

Saying that the government is responsible for our personal financial state is like saying "they" are responsible. I know that you've heard of the many things that "they" say, right? "They" often come up in this type of scenario:

"Hey, did you hear about what happened?"
"No. What happened?"
"'They' said that everyone is going to be fired today!"
"Who is 'they?'"
"I don't know. I heard someone else talking and that's what 'they' were saying."

Do you see how vague "they" can sound? Now let's see how it would sound if I were talking to you, and this was your argument.

Me: Why are you always broke and constantly borrowing money to make ends meet?

You: Well, "they" don't want me to succeed in life. "They" have all of the money for themselves. You know "they" make it hard out here for people like me.

Me: Who is "they"?

You: You know who "they" are. Don't play crazy!

Me: No, I really don't know who "they" are.

You: You know... the government!

Me: Did any one specific person tell you that?

You: No. I just know.

Does this dialogue sound silly or what? If you are placing the responsibility for the majority of your financial problems on the government, you are simply in denial. Yes, in some historical instances, the government has limited certain groups of people from benefiting from opportunities for contracts and jobs based on their race or gender. However, to resolve in your mind that you are restricted from prospering in a 21st century capitalistic society because of some unidentifiable entity that you've never personally encountered is a weak excuse for staying in poverty.

This type of thinking is characteristic of a poverty mentality. If you think like this, then it is highly likely that you have a sense of entitlement, and you feel like someone else is responsible for your life and the quality of it. WAKE UP! YOU are responsible! Blaming the government, the President or any other elected official for the state of your personal finances is a blatant attempt to avoid taking responsibility for your own financial affairs.

Your Parents – Some among us will choose to place the responsibility for our financial shortcomings on our parents. Many believe that it is the role of the parents to teach their children how to properly manage their finances. I personally agree with this belief; however, it is difficult to teach something to others that you do not personally know yourself.

Many of our parents were never properly taught how to manage their resources in a way that would lead to building generational wealth. Unfortunately, those same parents never took it upon themselves to learn how to systematically build wealth. Therefore, the expectation of these parents to teach their children wealth-building principles and personal financial management is somewhat unrealistic. Instead, the lessons that these parents will pass down will be those of poor financial stewardship.

I grew up in a single-parent household, and I was the third of six children. My father lived in another state and would provide for me on an as-needed basis. My mother rarely had any excess money. Therefore, the most that I was ever taught about money as a child was simply to "save money." I wasn't taught about *why* it was so important to save money, *how* to save money, or how to invest money in order to build wealth.

What I experienced was a lifestyle of struggling in order to make ends meet. We were living from check to check. We constantly robbed Peter to pay Paul. Then, we would ask Paul if we could borrow half of what we had just paid him in order to repay Peter. This was the normal money cycle in my childhood household.

It has been said that children retain more of what they *see* than what they *hear*. In essence, more is *caught* than *taught*. That was most definitely the case for me as I observed how money worked in my home. I never experienced any savings taking place in my home; saving money was more of a theory than a reality. However, as an adult, it was not acceptable for me to rely solely on the teachings of my parents on how to manage my money. There are far too many educational and teaching resources available about stewardship and money management for me to feel justified in blaming my poor money management habits on my parents' lack of teaching.

Certainly, there are many more scapegoats than the government and parents that people have chosen to place the burden of the blame for their financial misfortunes upon, but I do not have the time to list them all. I'm sure that you can think of something or someone else that may have played a major role in helping to shape your mentality and attitude about finances. Their influence may have helped you to get to where you are today.

Take a moment to reflect on someone or something that you feel may have caused or at least played a role in your lack of financial prosperity. Once you've identified the culprit, forgive the person or entity. Forgiving is an important step here, because until you're able to release whatever has been holding you back because of your feelings of anger, resentment, disappointment, guilt, etc., you will always want to reach back and blame them again. You have to deal with that situation once and for all in order to move to the next step. *"In order to move from where you are, you first have to deal with where you are."* – Dr. Dana Carson, MBA, Financial Stewardship Expert

> *"In order to move from where you are, you first have to deal with where you are."*
> **– Dr. Dana Carson, MBA, Financial Stewardship Expert**

FACING REALITY: YOU ARE RESPONSIBLE FOR WHERE YOU ARE

At some point, we have to accept responsibility for our own mistakes. We can't go through life being the victim. It's so easy to simply say, "It's not my fault," and remain in your current condition. Truthfully, it may *not* always be your fault; however it is now your responsibility to address and resolve the issue that you have been left to deal with, like it or not. If you fell off the side of a boat into the ocean, and it was clear that you fell because someone else deliberately pushed you, (it was clearly someone else's fault) would you attempt to swim to safety, or would you use your last breaths to cry out, "It's *not my fault!*" as you slowly drown, gasping for the precious air you need to survive? You must come to the realization that you have a lot of personal responsibility with where you are in life and that where you are in life is based upon the decisions that YOU have made. Once you own up to the fact that where you are is YOUR responsibility, then the process of fixing the long-term problem begins and you can start addressing the issue with the right perspective.

Chapter Six

START VIEWING YOUR OBSTACLES AS OPPORTUNITIES

On your journey towards unlocking your money mind, be warned: you will encounter many obstacles along the way. However, obstacles do not mean inevitable failure; it's all about how you handle them!

Let's first start by defining obstacles and opportunities:

- An obstacle is a thing or thought that blocks one's way or prevents or hinders progress. An obstacle can appear as a physical object or a mental thought. For the sake of our discussion, as it relates to your money mentality, we will be speaking strictly of mental obstacles.

- An opportunity is a good chance to advance or make progress towards a favorable or advantageous circumstance. Unlike obstacles, opportunities are almost always introduced to the mind first in the form of a thought.

Sometimes, what initially appears to be an obstacle may really be an opportunity! However, in order to see past the obstacle and view it as an opportunity, we must first change our perspective. There is a story in the Bible (John 5:1-8) in which Jesus addressed the mentality of a man at the pool of Bethesda. This man was paralyzed and could not provide for himself. He relied on others to take care of him and assist him with day-to-day functions.

In the culture, there was believed to be an occurrence once a year when the Angel of the Lord would come and stir the water in the pool. Whoever got into the water first would be healed of his sickness and disease. Depending on one's perspective, the stirring of the water could either be viewed as an obstacle or an opportunity.

Jesus encounters the lame man by the pool and engages in a dialogue with him. The man begins to tell Jesus about all of the times that he has tried to get into the pool to be healed, but someone always beat him to the water before he reached the pool (obstacle). Jesus, clearly seeing this as an unacceptable response, asked this man who had been laying on his mat for over 38 years an interesting question: "Do you want to be healed?" (opportunity). The man's internal response was likely something similar to, *"What do you think, Man? I've been lying here all my life waiting on my chance to get healed!"*

In essence, by asking the man if he wanted to be healed, Jesus was trying to say that there was no valid excuse for him still being lame for all of these years. If he truly wanted to be healed, he would have found a way to take advantage of the many opportunities that were presented to get the healing he needed. Think about it: the man had *38 years* of excuses!

At the core of this dialogue, Jesus was addressing the man's mentality. For example, there was nothing that said that the healing was limited to only one person. According to the story, it simply said that the first one into the water was guaranteed a healing, but it did not say that the second, third and fourth would *not* be healed.

Then, Jesus said something incredible to the man: "Rise, take up your bed and walk!" This is a powerful statement if you allow yourself to hear it correctly. Remember, this guy was *paralyzed*! Jesus ignored his current condition, totally disregarded his circumstances, and spoke directly to his faith. In doing so, Jesus gave the man three direct orders.

First, He told him to rise—to get up. He essentially gave the man permission to override his current physical limitations by faith. You will notice that at this point of the dialogue, the man has already had a change of mentality. How can we tell? Because he didn't respond to Jesus' command to get up with, *"Man, can't you see that I'm paralyzed?!"* Instead, he instantly stood on his feet.

The second order was for him to take up his bed. The bed speaks to the place of comfort and rest to which the man had become accustomed. Jesus was telling him that he could no longer live in such a state, being comfortable with his current condition. The bed could also be symbolic of the fact that the man had been at rest, inactive and dependent upon others for assistance all of his life. In light of his new ability to stand on his own power without the assistance of others, he no longer needed the bed because he would not be in this position again.

> There is no excuse for people (especially American citizens) to remain broke and impoverished all of their adult life.

The third order was to walk. Jesus told the man to do something that he had never done before. In other words, Jesus commanded the man to make progress towards new endeavors now that he was no longer held hostage by his physical and mental limitations.

I say to you that there is no excuse for people (especially American citizens) to remain broke and impoverished all of their adult life. There have been too many opportunities that have come your way. I say to you, according to your faith, get up (get out of your place of comfort)! Take up your bed (what you've depended on for years) and walk (make progress towards new endeavors and ventures)! You don't have to stay in the financial condition you're in for the rest of your life!

The man at this pool of Bethesda had one conversation with Jesus, and it *totally* changed his life forever. After he received this life-changing miracle, he was instantly met with resistance by haters. Instead of the people around him celebrating his new life and the opportunities he now had, they chose to question why he was walking and carrying his bed at a time when it was not appropriate according to their tradition. They had little appreciation for the fact that he was no longer dependent upon others for help.

I like his new disposition though. He simply replied, "He who made me well said to me, 'Take up your bed and walk'" (verse 11). In essence, the man said to his haters that someone with a higher authority than them gave him permission to change his condition, and he was not going to allow these people or their rules to deny him this opportunity!

It is obvious that the man was appreciative of the new life and liberty that he now had, because a few verses later (verse 14) the Bible says that Jesus found him in the temple (the house of worship). To show gratitude for what he had received from Jesus, the man became an evangelist and began to tell people about the Man who made him well (verse 15).

As you make the transition in your life and become independent of credit, debt, friends and family for financial support, you will encounter people that will not like "the new you." Do not become discouraged when this happens. Certain people are used to help you reach certain points in life. After you've reached that point, their portion of your life's journey is over, and you will need to meet new friends and associates to help you to go through the next phase of life.

Chapter Seven

YOUR MONEY HAS YOUR PERSONALITY

"Personal financial management is 80% behavior and 20% head knowledge."
- Dave Ramsey, Radio Host, Author and Financial Advisor

There has been extensive research conducted in the field of psychology that suggests that we all function according to a combination of four dominant personality types, also known as "temperaments." The studies suggest that there are common characteristics associated with each one of the four personalities. I will briefly explain the four temperaments, or personality types, using the DiSC model (an industry standard that provides training on the personality types). Just for fun, I will also throw in a vehicle that's symbolic of the personality of each temperament. After learning about the different temperaments, you will be able to identify your own personality type and understand how your personality type may have a strong influence on your financial decision-making and personal money management.

TYPE 1: DOMINANT (AKA "BOSS HOG")

This temperament type tends to be very aggressive by nature. They are what some would call "go getters" because of their intense level of drive and determination. Boss Hogs are considered to be goal driven and very task oriented. They can tend to be un-emotional and insensitive towards the feelings of others. People of this personality type are likely to start their own business, become an entrepreneur, or serve in a leadership capacity in an organization. They typically like to make the rules and are stubborn when it comes to following someone else's rules.

Personality in a Nutshell: Egocentric, direct, daring, domineering, demanding

Vehicle Type: Hummer

Personality Pros: Aggressive, decisive, confident, optimistic

Personality Cons: Insensitive, impatient, defiant, can't maintain long-term close relationships

Greatest Fear: Being taken advantage of. They are very skeptical of the motives of others. They feel there's always an angle to the intentions of others.

Most Likely Career Choices: Business owner, investor, CEO, law enforcement

Money Management Style: Boss Hogs are risk takers and will try many different ventures looking for success. They will likely start a small business and will not be afraid to invest their money into the business. They will also invest the money of others into their business without regard for the risk of loss associated with starting the business. They believe passionately in their vision, and they are willing to put it all on the line in order to accomplish or realize the manifestation of the vision. The Boss Hog will make long-term plans for success and will develop a strategy to execute the plan. Typically, the Boss Hog will make risky investments without having the details necessary to determine if the investment will be profitable. They make money decisions based on their optimism (especially when the investment idea originates with them). They are the embodiment of the Nike slogan "Just Do It." Many times, this type of risk-taking behavior leads to either huge success or huge loss. The Boss Hog lives by the motto: "Go BIG, or Go HOME!"

TYPE 2: INFLUENTIAL (AKA "PARTY PLEASER")

This personality type is the one that most would consider to be "the life of the party." When they show up to an environment, it suddenly becomes a lot more entertaining. It's like they possess an inner happiness that can't be contained, and at any given moment, that happiness will explode on the scene and cause others to loosen up and have fun. The Party Pleaser has an outgoing personality and can get along with nearly anyone. They burst with energy, and are always fun to be around. All things are possible to this person.

Personality in a Nutshell: Enthusiastic, gregarious, persuasive, impulsive, emotional

Vehicle Type: Lamborghini

Personality Pros: Energetic, enthusiastic, creative, optimistic

Personality Cons: Un-organized, un-reliable, inconsistent, immature

Greatest Fear: Social rejection. They can easily fall into depression if they perceive that they are not liked by people. They are often very sensitive to how others perceive them.

Most Likely Career Choices: Musical artist, sports athlete, entertainer, salesman, party planner

Money Management Style: Party Pleasers tend to be big spenders. They live to impress others. You may know them as "The Joneses.'" They will likely spend much more than they earn in order to maintain a false image for their friends, family, and practically anyone that will look. They are very budget resistant and see a budget as being too restrictive for their "free-spirited" personality. Living on the edge is normal for this personality type. They can sometimes confuse their natural optimism with godly faith. Consequently, they enter into situations that are very unrealistic and unattainable; however, because they can't distinguish the difference between their optimism and faith that is based upon what God actually said, they commit to something with unrelenting passion and belief. Party Pleasers are usually not money savvy when it comes to long-term investments and wealth building. To them, this takes too much planning, and such things are too far up the road to be concerned with today. The Party Pleaser lives by the motto: "I'm living for the weekend!"

TYPE 3: STEADINESS (AKA "FREE WILLY")

The Free Willy person is the team player. They will be the mediator of any group and will seek to bring everyone to some sort of happy medium. They provide balance to any team, and they are slow to get upset. This person is your loyal friend and likes consistency. They are usually willing to give of their resources to help others or support a cause. The Free Willy personality type is oftentimes most content with whatever condition they are in, as long as there is peace and no conflict. Lots of contention and arguing are detrimental to this person, and for them it is always taken personally. While others may have the ability to argue or strongly disagree over an issue and move on like it never happened, the Free Willy is grieved by heated arguments, and they tend to internalize the conflict and assume that the conflict was their fault. Consequently, they will not rest until the conflict is resolved and everyone is happy again. As long as there is friction between them and someone else, they will not be at peace.

Personality in a Nutshell: Passive, patient, loyal, predictable, team player

Vehicle Type: Volvo

Personality Pros: Dependable, reliable, supportive, consistent, safe

Personality Cons: Indecisive, rebellious, stubborn, passive

Greatest Fear: Instability is the greatest fear of this personality type. They do not like to change once they have gotten comfortable in their ways. They like established, dependable jobs where they know they can work until retirement.

Most Likely Career Choices: Vice President, teacher, middle manager, counselor, executive assistant

Money Management Style: The Free Willy personality type is willing to take calculated risks in moderation. They are not ultra conservative; however they are not big risk takers either. There is a strong tendency for these people to give of themselves and their resources to others in order for the others to succeed. When it comes to their own projects, they are less likely to invest a lot into themselves or their projects. They are very critical of their ideas and are doubtful when it comes to launching something on their own. Because of the team player inherent in this Free Willy personality type, they find joy in helping others to succeed and be happy. Therefore, they will likely give away most of their money and time with no return in mind. They tend to be very sympathetic with people and are often taken advantage of as a result of their free spirit. The Free Willy may feel a certain level of guilt for becoming successful when others whom they love and associate with are not. Consequently, they end up remaining "normal" or "average" for the sake of others instead of maximizing their life and potential. They are of the motto from the late Rodney King: "Can't we all just get along?"

TYPE 4: CONSCIENTIOUS (AKA "PENNY PINCHER")

The Penny Pincher is the ultimate perfectionist. They are very calculated and detailed. It is extremely rare for the Penny Pincher to make a decision about anything without a thorough analysis of all of the factors associated with the outcome of the decision. They also tend to be very legalistic and rule driven. This personality type is not usually motivated by the opinions of others or their social status. They tend to be very isolated and self-contained. Typically, they do not have a lot of friends in their social circles due to their independence.

Personality in a Nutshell: Perfectionist, accurate, conservative, diplomatic, systematic

Vehicle type: Honda Civic

Personality Pros: Attentive, self-motivated, analytical, discipline

Personality Cons: Perfectionist, fact-driven, rule-driven, overly critical

Greatest Fear: The fear of being wrong is the greatest fear of this personality type. Penny Pinchers are so inundated with facts and research to the point that when the data they rely so heavily upon is challenged or wrong, it crushes their entire world. Penny Pinchers feel that they are right 100% of the time, and if in the event they are wrong, it's not their fault because they misunderstood the data or information.

Most Likely Career Choices: Accountant, attorney, doctor, engineer, architect

Money Management Style: Frugal. Frugal. Frugal. The Penny Pincher is what some would call a "tight wad"—they are not risk takers by any stretch of the imagination! They are very calculated and detailed when it comes to spending money. Most will have accurate records of their financial history for the past five years within reach of their desk. Penny Pinchers are budget-conscious, and they believe that it is totally reckless to not have a 20-page spreadsheet of their finances. Some might also refer to them as "nerds." They tend to be plainly dressed in very conservative attire with no hint of fashion. They will likely drive a car that gets exceptional gas mileage.

Penny Pinchers have a set amount of money for every expense associated with their uneventful life-style. They typically are not generous in giving of their resources unless it is for tax purposes, because they receive a direct benefit from making such contributions. When it comes to investing their money, Penny Pinchers are likely to find comfort in low-risk mutual funds, or investments with little-to-no risk of total loss of the initial investment. Retirement is of high priority for the Penny Pincher personality type because they are independent and do not want to have to rely on anyone for assistance in their senior years. Therefore, they place a great deal of importance on saving and planning for retirement. Because Penny Pinchers tend to be very systematic in their approach to life, they are very likely to be successful with building wealth in the long term if they implement the tools early enough in life that will lead to a slow but certain accumulation of wealth.

DOMINANT & SECONDARY PERSONALITY TYPES

I took the time to share these various personalities or temperament types with you in hopes that you would discover a little more about yourself than you were even aware of concerning the way you function and how it affects your money management.

Each of us has both a dominant personality type and a secondary personality type. Take a moment to review the information on the four personalities and then identify which type you think is your dominant and secondary personality type. Then, look at the money management styles associated with each personality type to see if your money management styles match. It should be pretty accurate!

I know you're probably asking "*What do I do with this new insight about myself and my tendencies in managing money?*" There are no specific answers that I can give to you in this book due to the multiple personality blends that exist; a solution that might work for one would not necessarily work for others. Additionally, certain considerations like one's culture, (behavioral norms and acceptable practices of environment) nature (natural behavioral tendencies based on your DNA) and your nurture (your upbringing, experiences and exposure) must also be factored into treating each individual's money management solution, for each of these things helps to paint a true picture of who you are. Because no two people are exactly the same, no solutions to personality-based money management styles will be exactly the same.

However, what I can tell you is this: if you follow the plans laid out in this book and embrace the mental keys that I offer for your mental and financial freedom, your personality type will not be as big of a determining factor when it comes to the success of your long-term wealth-building strategy!

Chapter Eight

WHERE DO I START ON THE RECOVERY PROCESS?

We are now at the point of no return! Hopefully, you've been enjoying the book up to this point. I know you're probably asking, *"When are we going to talk about building wealth?"* I know it may seem like we've covered a lot of things dealing with our mindset —and we have—but remember, as I said earlier, this book deals with more than just the numbers behind wealth building.

I've provided you with two quotes thus far, and if you took the time to read them, you will agree that both of them are extremely powerful. The first one was from Dr. Dana Carson, who stated that we have to first *identify* where we are in order to *move from* where we are to where we want to be. The second one was from Dave Ramsey, who stated that personal finances are 80% *behavior* and 20% *knowledge*. A major factor in moving from where you are to where you want to be with building wealth is how you think. Thus, up to this point, I have spent a lot of time trying to help you to identify some of the mental roadblocks that you may be dealing with in your wealth building journey.

THE MONEY MENTALITY RECAP

Thus far, we have discussed some of the mental keys to unlocking your mind in order to unlock your money, placing you on the right track to begin building wealth. These include the following 8 Mental Keys:

1. The enemy is in your mind!

2. Learn from the mistakes of others!

3. Be willing to throw out old thinking!

4. If you're fat, say "I'm fat!" Don't lie to yourself!

5. Cash is your friend. Take advantage of the relationship!

6. Stop overeating!

7. Change your perspective!

8. Stop looking for someone to blame!

Additionally, we have discussed the necessity of having the proper foundational understanding about resources: that it all belongs to God and that we are only stewards. Then, we briefly identified our primary and secondary personality types and how they influence the ways in which we tend to handle money. At this point, we are now about to enter into learning some concrete action items that are necessary to get you financially fit!

Remember earlier when I said that we are all members of the same gym, running on the perpetual earn-to-consume treadmill? I also stated that there was no contract obligating us to stay and remain a member of that gym. Well, here is the point at which we decide whether we want to remain a member of the gym or whether we want to terminate our contract permanently!

The next section of the book will equip you with practical ways to reach financial freedom and empower you with practical strategies to build your wealth. It all begins with my 10-Step Redemption Plan!

10-STEP REDEMPTION PLAN

The number 10 in biblical numerology (the study of numbers) represents the number of redemption. Redemption, in a theological context, means deliverance from sin or bondage, and it can also refer to salvation. To redeem something is simply to recover it. Thus, for our purposes, we will define redemption as "the act of recovering that which was lost", which for most people will be time lost that could have been used to build wealth with your resources.

It is my goal to establish for you a practical yet holistic 10-Step Redemption Plan that will completely re-orient the way you view, save, give and invest your money from this point on in your life. It's never too late to redeem something in your life. Just as salvation doesn't have a expiration date or a "use by" date on it (with the exception of death), neither does an action plan to get your financial life in order.

As you prepare for this next leg of the journey, keep an open mind as you implement the steps prescribed. Consider the 10-Step Redemption Plan that follows to be a general prescription for a common problem. I understand that because different people may be in different stages of developing their finances, some of the information may not be 100% applicable to every individuals situation today; however, the general principles of each step can be applied in some way to your personal financial management, whatever the stage of your financial development, and if nothing else, they can serve as a reminder of what steps to take in the future.

WARNING

*Do not skip any portion of the following steps. I know that you will be tempted to do so, but skipping even **one** step could cause serious setbacks to your financial success!*

THE 10-STEP REDEMPTION PLAN

Step #1. Establish Your Motive

What is a motive? A motive can be defined as the goal or object of a person's actions. A motive can also be defined as something that causes a person to act in a certain way or manner. In simple terms, a motive answers the "why" behind our actions. Now that we are clear on what a motive is, we must establish a clear motive for building wealth.

I've learned that building wealth is not easy. If it was an easy thing to do, *everyone* would be wealthy! I think that at this point, we can establish that there are certain disciplines that are required to build wealth. However, before we get to the more difficult disciplines, we must have a clear reason for wanting to change our habits and adopt a totally new mindset surrounding wealth building.

Taking the time to establish a crystal-clear motive for your desired outcome allows you to continue to press forward when everything inside of you wants to find an excuse to quit and go back to your comfortable, old financial habits.

*Scenario: Your child becomes sick and is diagnosed with a terminal illness. The doctor tells you that your child has 6 months to live unless the child receives the cure within that timeframe. There is a cure that exists, but the cost is $15,000 for the medicine. This gives you 6 months to come up with the money, but the stipulation is that you can't borrow the money from anyone. If you woke up tomorrow and this was your reality, would you come up with that money some kind of way? Of course you would! How? You would realize that you eat out too much, that cable is unnecessary, and that you spend too much money on shopping, golfing, entertainment, etc. Some kind of way, you would find $15,000 for your child. Why? Because you would be **motivated** to save your child! Your income didn't change, your habits did! You simply changed your habits because there was something of more importance at stake, and making the sacrifice to give up things that were not critical to your life was easy because of your new motivation!*

Hopefully, this will never be your reality. However, do you see what happened? The same sense of urgency you would feel in the preceding scenario is the same sense of urgency and focus you should have when it comes to saving and building wealth.

If you have plans to save for a car, home, wedding, vacation, business, etc. you should have a visual aid (picture of the item, progress chart, or something you can see) that will keep you motivated. Again, this will assist you with staying focused on saving the money for whatever it is you want. Use this visual aid as a constant reminder of why you're making the sacrifices you're making. In Proverbs 29:18, the Bible states "Where there is no vision, the people perish (cast off restraint)." Simply put, when you don't have a visual of what you are pursuing, the parameters and disciplines that you need to accomplish your desired outcome will be tossed aside, and you will become unfocused. Therefore, keep a visual representation of the vision in front of you!

Step #2. Identify Your Kryptonite

If you have the ability to read this book, then I'm certain that you have seen at least one version of the movie *Superman*. Superman was a superhero who possessed enormous amounts of power and could do things that would be impossible for normal humans to do. He could fly at the speed of light, deflect bullets when he was being showered by gunfire, be thrown through brick buildings without sustaining any injuries, etc. Nonetheless, Superman, with all of his super powers, still had a weak spot. His weakness was a mineral called "kryptonite." Anytime he would encounter kryptonite, it would instantly drain him of his super powers and render him almost completely helpless. However, the farther he got away from the kryptonite, the more power he was able to regain.

Each of us has our own financial kryptonite: that which weakens and drains us of our resources. For some people, their kryptonite may be their family members constantly in need of loans and support. For others, it could be overspending as they try to keep up with the Joneses. Then, there are others whose kryptonite may be gambling, drinking, drug abuse, relationships, golfing, shopping, eating out, playing the lottery, etc.!

We must all take time to identify our own individual sources of kryptonite that keep us stagnant and powerless when it comes to building wealth. Once you identify what drains you, get as far away from it as possible.

Superman didn't destroy the kryptonite. Instead, he simply created distance between himself and that which drained his strength. I ask you today, what is *your* kryptonite? Only you can answer this question. Take a moment to identify your kryptonite before moving on to the next step.

Step #3. Create Some Accountability

Having someone that you're accountable to in this process will help you to maximize your wealth-building efforts. Trust me: the time will come when you will be ready to throw in the towel, making a conscious decision to abort this whole 10-Step Redemption Plan due to the complexity and difficulty that it entails. If this is a new endeavor for you and you've never attempted to establish a budget, save money, invest, etc., it will be difficult at first. But again, always remember this: if building wealth was easy, *everyone* would be wealthy!

Initially, the process will be painful. Results may be dismal. Progress may be slow. You will swear that this plan simply doesn't work. Others will likely jump on the bandwagon with you and support your desire to abort the process.

If and when this happens, remember this... IT'S WORKING! When your broke friends see what you're doing and tell you it's stupid, say to yourself, "IT'S WORKING!" If your broke family members start saying things like, "You think you're better than us," say to yourself, "IT'S WORKING!"

This is the point at which you will be most vulnerable. Your personality type will emerge, rearing its head right in the middle of this process and demand to be heard.

- The Boss Hog will become frustrated with the challenge because it wasn't his idea and will begin to say things like, "This is stupid!"

- The Party Pleaser will simply want to abort the process due to the perceived social rejection from friends and family who are not on board with them.

- The Free Willy will likely want to give in to the status quo and conform to the environment because no one else is on board with them in this new endeavor. They don't want the team to alienate them because they are changing.

- The Penny Pincher will likely become over-obsessed with getting to the end and knowing "exactly" what the end result will be. Therefore they will want to research whether this "stuff" is accurate.

If you start to feel any of these thoughts during the process, remember: IT'S WORKING! No one likes change. We resist change constantly. However, we must also acknowledge that if we do not change, we cannot move forward.

Step #4. Make the Commitment to Yourself, to Your Family and to God

> *Thinking leads to feelings, which lead to how we act. What I think determines how I will feel, and how I feel will determine how I will act.*

"*Thinking leads to feelings, which lead to how we act. What I think determines how I will feel, and how I feel will determine how I will act.*" – Eugene Van Kramburg, Bishop of ROCK World Outreach Ministries, S. Africa

This step is critical to your success. In order for you to make this transition success-fully, you will have to settle in your mind that this is something you're going to pursue relentlessly. It's often easier to convince other people to stick to some-thing than it is to convince ourselves.

You know how to sell the story to others of how you're going to do this and that, but after the conver-sation is over, the realities of your lack of discipline set in, and before long, all of the talk ends up being just that: talk! Therefore, in order for it to become a reality, the talk will have to be accompanied by spe-cific action plans complete with timelines. Commit to giving this effort all that you've got, and resolve that you will not give up!

It will be up to you to resolve in your own mind that *this is worth the commitment, and the payoff is worth the sacrifice.* In fact, read this statement aloud wherever you are right now: **This is worth the commitment, and the payoff is worth the sacrifice!**

When you finally convince yourself that you are serious and committed to the process, the next step is to commit to your family or those closest to you. By doing this, you add an extra layer of accountability to the process. Your family should help to keep you on task and not give room for the many excuses that you will come up with throughout the process. In fact, you might want to even give your family permission to slap you every time you try to abort the process!

Warning: You should be extremely selective about which family members to share your new commitment with, because your family can cause you to forfeit your future by infusing your renewed mind with old thinking, habits, and traditions. You can't put new wine into old wineskins. Simply put, your renewed outlook on money management and wealth building is highly active and filled with intense actions designed to take you from one place to the next. Despite your best efforts to share them, some of the people in your life will not be able to contain them; the principles will be too intense for them to handle, so they will not be able to relate to you or your new mentality! Therefore, trying to put this content into a family member with an old mentality could possibly destroy the relationship. Purchase a copy of this book for them to read before you expose yourself to the potential for frustration from people who love you, and in their minds, are only trying to help you.

Finally, commit to God. This is the most powerful form of accountability. Unlike your own mental commitment or your commitment to your family, this commitment to God has a power with which the others cannot compete. For example, you are the only one that knows the manipulative ploys that you use on yourself that give you permission to abort your goals. Then, no family member will be able to ultimately keep you on task long term because you know that at some point, you can talk your way out of being accountable to them.

> *God will not make you do anything against your free will.*

However, because you know that God is all-knowing and that there's nothing that you can hide from Him, you are much more likely to stick to a commitment that you make to Him. There have been documented stories of people who have lost enormous amounts of weight after attempting several diets and weight loss programs without success. However, they claim that after including prayer and allowing God to help them meet their weight loss goals, they were very successful in losing the weight.

God is a great accountability partner. However, YOU still have to be ultimately responsible for seeing the process to completion. God will not make you do anything against your free will. He doesn't make you accept Him, so surely He won't make you commit to staying on budget, saving money, or building wealth.

Special note: This process will take some time. You will not see instant results, but over time, the process will work and you will begin to see manifestations take place in every aspect of your life.

Step #5: Create an "Emergency" Fund

The very first money decision that needs to be made in order to put you in a better position for unlocking your money is to set aside $1,000 for emergencies. This money should be cash, and you should be able to access it fairly quickly. Keeping it in a traditional savings account at a bank is sufficient for this initial stage. You might be wondering, *"How do I come up with $1,000?"* The answer is simple. Save it. Sell some stuff that you don't use. Be creative. We will talk more about this a little later. Keep reading.

For the average household, $1,000 should be sufficient to cover any small emergency. By having this emergency fund, you are now in a position to remove the credit card as your security crutch. There will come a time when the car will not start, the air conditioner will go out right in the heat of summer, or some type of emergency repair will be needed around the house. Since most families live from paycheck to paycheck and do not have any designated money set aside for emergencies, when an emergency arises, the only funds they have available to them is a credit card. By having this emergency fund in place, you can avoid using a credit card as a backup plan.

Step #6. Prioritize Your Budget

Everyone hates the word "budget." To some people, the word budget means "I'm broke", or "I can't have something I want." On the contrary, the word budget should be viewed as more of a guide that you establish to tell your money where to go instead of always wondering where your money went.

I believe that the word "budget" got a bad reputation because many parents used the budget as a means to deny the purchase of something we wanted as children, and therefore the negativity associated with the budget has carried over into our adult lives. Simply put, all a budget should be is a plan that outlines what money is going where. Hey, it's *your* budget. *You* create it, so *you* control what goes on with it!

I believe that another reason why some people are afraid of the word "budget" is because they are afraid that they will have to face the reality that they are living way above their means. For some people, that's a little too much reality to handle; therefore, they ignore it and continue living like they were: broke and in denial. Unfortunately, this attitude will have to change if you plan on unlocking your money so that you can start building wealth. You can't behave like an ostrich by sticking your head into a hole in the ground and acting as if the problem doesn't exist. The longer you keep your big head buried in the ground ignoring the problem, the longer and more difficult your process of getting a handle on your finances and starting your journey to wealth building will be.

Also note that your budget should be specific – down to zero. What I mean by this is that after you sit down and identify what you plan to spend, every single dollar should have a name and a *purpose*. All of your income, regardless of the source, should have an *assignment* as soon as it enters your life. Leaving money that does not have an assignment or purpose tends to create a perfect atmosphere for impulse spending.

Your budget should consist of the following:

Tithes and Offerings (Malachi 3:8-10) – Ten percent of your gross earnings should be taken right off the top and given to your ministry to support God's work through the local church (remember our "First Things First" discussion earlier). Offerings should be given to the local church as well; however there is no specific pre-determined amount. Offerings are free will gifts, which means that you should give them out of your love for and relationship with God.

Remember the story of the $36,000 that I blew earlier in the book? I explained that outside of giving to my church, I didn't know where the rest of the money went. Well, that dollar amount with the tithe and offering combined was over $7,200. I knew where $7,200 was, because it instantly went to my church before anything else had a chance to convince me that I could put it to better use elsewhere. One of the things that I knew then and still practice now was to never violate God with my (His) money.

Shelter – You must have a safe place to live. Therefore, you should take care of your housing expenses (mortgage/rent, utilities, insurance, etc.). If this portion of your budget is disproportionately large, then you may need to consider adjusting your choice of where you live. Downgrading your lifestyle may be a necessity in order to put you in position to build wealth. You should determine what you can afford for housing based on your income. I recommend staying under 30% of your monthly income for housing expenses.

Food – This category is known to send people into shock when they realize how much money they spend on eating out, between-meal snacks, coffee, specialty drinks, alcohol, etc. For budgeting purposes, food is primarily considered grocery store food that needs to be cooked. This food is called "survival food" by many during this stage. We're not eating steak and seafood much during this process. I suggest foods that you can cook in bulk like spaghetti, soups, pasta dishes, etc. This way, you can eat more than once off of the same money you spent to prepare the meal, because there will be leftovers. This will also help to reduce your need to buy food at work, because you can simply take your lunch with you.

When it comes to dining out, I recommend limiting these occasions to once per week on a day that you determine. If you can't go "cold turkey" on dining out, then at least use this once-a-week occasion as the day that you have your favorite meal at your favorite restaurant (within reason). I want the budget to work, so I understand that there has to be some wiggle room in it, or else you will get frustrated and abort the process. With that said, _keep in mind the big picture_ of where you are headed financially. Eating out doesn't mean steak and lobster meals with shrimp fondue as an appetizer and a $10 glass of wine. Moderation is the key!

Clothing – This expense will vary depending on what type of work you do. For example, if you are in a line of work in which you wear a uniform daily (military, police, fireman, etc.), then you could save a lot in this category. However, if you work in a professional environment where the company dress code requires your attire to be business or business casual, then you will need to allocate more in the clothing category of the budget. However, again, _keep in mind the big picture_! Just because your job requires that you dress in business casual attire doesn't mean that you have to shop at Neiman's or Saks Fifth Avenue for your clothes. Your clothing budget should be watched carefully, because it can easily be manipulated and justified in the name of, "I'm a professional, so I have to dress like this to impress my clients." Custom tailor-made suits are not what I'm referring to here as acceptable clothing to include in the budget. Also, keep in mind that you may not need to fund this part of your budget on a monthly basis.

Transportation – In our society, it is nearly impossible to function without reliable transportation. There are some locations where the public transportation system is sufficient, but the overwhelming majority of people rely on their own private transportation to get to work, school, shop, transport children, and go about their daily lives. Therefore, transportation, gas, maintenance, etc. need to be factored into your monthly budget.

I have discovered a secret that I will share with you. However, you must promise that you will not tell anyone you know about our little secret. Here we go. You can actually have reliable transportation _without_ having a car payment! Shhhhh! Did you know that? I know, I know: it is considered taboo in America to have a car without a payment. Many people believe that the rich are the only people who can afford a car without a payment. On the contrary, most of the people we would normally consider rich have a huge car payment due to their extravagant vehicle choices. However, wealthy people choose quality used cars and pay cash for them. That's what you will do from now on if you follow my advice.

There are certain things in America that many people believe have to coexist with each other, or it's not considered authentic American. It's like having breakfast without orange juice, a hamburger with no cheese, or a student without a loan. If you have fallen for the myth of not being able to have a car without a payment, then in the next step, I will help you become a myth-buster. In the meantime, budget for your car payments and the associated maintenance related to the vehicle.

6. Miscellaneous Expenses – Other things that need to be included in your budget are household items such as toiletries, pampering expenses (hair, nails, etc. in moderation), telephone services (home, cell, internet), vehicle repair, home repair, money for entertainment (in moderation, and only after all of the previous expenses have been taken care of), credit card bills, etc.

Step #7. Pay Off Debt

This step is absolutely critical to building wealth. Forbes Magazine did an interview with the 500 wealthiest people in America and asked them what their key to building wealth was. The number one response from all of the participants was "becoming and staying debt free." Debt is normally the biggest consumer of our income. Therefore, it is imperative that we rid ourselves of this bondage as soon as possible. We will spend a considerable amount of time on this step due to the grip that it has on most people.

In the Bible, Proverbs 22:7 says, *"The rich rule over the poor, and the borrower is slave to the lender."* In essence, when you borrow money from someone, the relationship dynamics change without your consent. You instantly enslave yourself to whomever it was who loaned you the money. Unlike the slavery system of the past in which many were forced into submission and oppression against their will, borrowing money is *a conscious decision* to walk into voluntary slavery.

Have you ever stopped to think about where the name "Master" Card comes from? I'm not simply picking on Master Card, because all credit cards are equally evil in my opinion. It just happens to be the one with the name that believes in full self-disclosure... Master! Debt is a brutal slave master. Debt is unemotional, insensitive, unforgiving, merciless, and it does not have the ability to be sympathetic with you. Debt is a principle-driven slave master. Simply put, if you use debt, you will become a slave to it.

How Do I Get Out of this Debt?

The first step to getting out of debt is to **STOP BORROWING MONEY!** Unlike the government, you can't simply print up more money when you get into a financial pitfall. Therefore, you have to commit to stop borrowing money every time you get into a financial bind or some new item grabs your attention and compels you to purchase it.

I recommend paying off your debts from smallest to largest. *"Heyyyy… wait a minute!"* you must be thinking. *"Shouldn't I pay off the one with the highest interest rate first?"* Paying off debt in the highest-to-lowest interest rate order is the common theory among economics professors, and strictly from an economics standpoint, it makes logical sense. However, we are not simply dealing with the numbers. This process is personal, and it involves your emotions.

To increase the likelihood of you completing the process of paying off your debts, I recommend paying the smallest debt off first so that you can see some progress, and therefore, stay motivated. As you pay off a small debt, you achieve a small victory, which then motivates you to pay off the next debt. However, while you are paying off the smallest debt first, continue to make minimum payments on your other debts.

As you pay off one debt, take all of the payments that you were making on the first debt, and then add them to the payment on the next smallest debt. Repeat this process with every debt you have. Eventually, you will be paying double and triple payments on one loan.

Now, you will have two things happening simultaneously. The first thing that you are doing is paying off your debts. The second thing that you are doing is freeing up your income, which is your largest wealth-building tool.

Are you beginning to see the logic behind doing it this way? Paying the smallest debts off first helps to build momentum, so that by the time you get to your last payment, you are dumping a large sum of money at the debt item, and it will be paid off sooner. The beauty of this formula for paying off your debts is that, if you notice, you are not taking any additional money from your operating budget. As you pay off each small debt, that money that you were paying is simply added to the next debt payment.

How do I pay off debt when I don't have any extra money?

If I'm correct, now you are asking, "My money is already tight, and I can barely pay my bills as it is. How am I supposed to get this ball rolling?" Great question! I'm so glad you asked, because I have the answer. Below are a few quick ways to get the ball rolling and gain some quick momentum:

Use the excess money you've saved from eating out less, eliminating your cable, etc. After you have streamlined your budget and cut out all non-necessity items, you should free up some extra money somewhere.

Have a garage sale. There are items lying around the house that you can sell to make some quick cash. I mean really... no, seriously... do you *need* 6 televisions? Those golf clubs haven't been used in years, and that underutilized $1,000 gym set in the garage is really taking up valuable space. By taking a critical look at some of the things lying around your house and selling them, you can jump start your debt reduction plan!

Pick up an extra job solely for paying down debt. This does not have to be a long-term deal; however, _keep in mind the big picture_ of what you're trying to accomplish. Don't be too proud to flip a burger, deliver a pizza, cut some lawns, wash some cars, work overtime at your current job, deliver a newspaper, etc.

If you employ these ideas and generate extra income to get the ball rolling, don't stop until the ball is big enough to sustain the momentum without the extra work.

In fact, once the ball is big enough, you will have likely become accustomed to the extra money and you may even want to hold on to your extra job a little longer. That's a personal choice. I'm all for it! If you have the opportunity to earn some extra income and it doesn't disrupt your values and beliefs, go for it!

All of your debts should be addressed in this step with the exception of your house. Because your home is typically a larger loan amount, you can save this for a later step in the process. By the time you make your final payment on your largest debt, you will feel like a champion – and you will be, so break out the *Rocky* theme music! You will officially be ranked in the top 10% of Americans in terms of wealth. No silly, you will not have millions of dollars in the bank, but there are very few people that can make the statement that they are debt free.

You will be well on your way to building some serious wealth now that you don't have any nagging monthly payments outside of basic household expenses. At this point, you will realize that the money you bring home from your job lasts a lot longer, and you have just given yourself a huge pay raise. CONGRATULATIONS CHAMP!

Step #8. Complete Your "Emergency" Fund

Now that you've slain the debt dragon, you are well on your way to financial freedom. The rest of the process will be much easier. At this point in the process, it's time to fully fund your emergency fund. All of that extra money that you have at your disposal now should make this a quick and painless process. A fully-funded emergency fund is considered to be three to six months of your household expenses. For most people, this figure will range anywhere from $6,000 to $12,000.

Take a breath and enjoy the feeling of having no payments outside of your home and having up to $12,000 sitting in the bank, free and clear. At this point in your journey, you will begin to notice weird things happening. For example, your level of stress will have decreased tremendously. You will not be easily frustrated by small, trivial things that people do. You will view your job as an opportunity to build wealth instead of it being an obligatory function that you must attend due to the massive amount of debt you have accumulated. You will notice that many of the things like clothing, jewelry, cars, and the other toys you once couldn't live without are not even attractive to you anymore.

At this stage, the freedom of being able to give like you want to and leaving an inheritance for your children becomes more important than the newest gadget, those new golf clubs, and the look that the other broke people give you when you pull up in your luxury vehicle. You will start to realize how shallow those things are in light of the big picture. Another weird experience that you will encounter is that you will not place as much value on what others think about you and your image. By now, you will have realized that *it was the image that you were trying to keep up* that had you in the financial mess you were in from the beginning. You will realize that the Joneses that you were trying to keep up with were broke – and very likely one to two paychecks away from the poor-house themselves. You will feel truly liberated after you have reached this point in the journey.

Step #9. Invest

Now that your emergency fund is fully funded and your income is free, you are in position to invest. I did not mention investing before this step because it would have been out of order – too premature. Many believe that you should invest in things that make money before you get out of debt. That sounds logical, right? Well, let's look at it a little closer.

Let's say you have $10,000 lying around in a savings account, but you also have $40,000 in debt consisting of a car payment, student loans and credit cards. Let's average the interest on all of your debts to an even 10%. Over a period of one year, you will have paid $4,000 in interest to the banks. You know as well as I do that there aren't many places in the market where you will earn a 10% rate of return. Surely you will not get that at a bank with their 0.03% rates. But, for the sake of argument, let's say you can get a 10% rate on your $10,000. That's good right? Let's see. Ultimately you will earn $1,000 in interest on your savings, while paying out $4,000 in interest to the bank. According to my math, you are negative $3,000 per year. Now, let's say you took that same $10,000 and paid it towards your debt. That would leave you with a balance of $30,000. In that same year, you will have only paid $3,000 in interest to the bank. Mathematically, you still earned/saved $1,000 in interest by not paying out $1,000 to the bank. In addition to the $1,000 that you just earned, you are now that much closer to having the loans paid off. By paying off the debt, you have just created an opportunity for your #1 wealth-building asset (which is your income) to be targeted towards building wealth for you and your family instead of building the bank's wealth. You decide which formula looks better.

Where should I invest?

Now that that's out of the way, let's continue on our journey to unlocking your money! By now, you're probably wondering, *"In what should I invest?"* I'm glad you asked. My recommendations are as follows:

Invest in Yourself: Conduct an inventory of the skills that you possess and determine whether or not you can enhance them in order to become more valuable to your clients. FYI: I believe that if you work for an organization as an employee, you should treat your job as if you are an independent contractor providing a service.

By adopting this mentality, you will never see yourself as "just another employee." You will also see an increase in your productivity because you no longer consider it an *obligation* to be at work; instead, you see your employment as an *opportunity* and a resource to build your wealth. Thus, you will notice that I used the word "client" earlier in this section instead of "employer."

Today, there are many avenues through which you can invest in yourself. One of the most common avenues is through higher learning at a college or university. I must caution you in regards to college, though. I believe that a college degree can be a valuable tool if it is focused properly and if there is an immediate use for the knowledge learned. Many people feel that by simply having a college degree, they will be guaranteed success. In today's job market, having a four-year undergraduate college degree is slowly becoming the equivalent of having a high school diploma.

The market is saturated with college graduates who are currently out of work or under-employed, so it will take more than just a degree to get an edge on the market. If the field of interest you want to pursue requires a degree, then investing in a college degree is a good investment. However, be cautious of the ever-increasing cost of college tuition. When choosing to increase your learning through college, you should be mindful of the return on investment (ROI). You must make a realistic assessment of how this investment in higher learning will directly impact your bottom line and what currently-closed doors will be opened as a result of this investment.

Another method of investing in yourself is through that of purchasing personal development materials from experts in your current field or the field you are interested in pursuing. Most of these experts have spent thousands of dollars and countless hours learning their trade. For a fraction of the cost of what they paid, you can learn some of the best methods to become successful in that field, paying perhaps only a few hundred dollars for what they paid thousands to learn. Seminars on the subject area that you are interested in are also great methods of increasing your value for a fraction of the cost.

In the workplace, promotions are usually based upon the value that you bring to the organization. The more valuable you are to the organization, the more money it will be willing to pay you. Thus, the next time you feel like you deserve a pay raise, consider what additional value you will provide for the organization before you ask for the raise. If you want more *out* of the organization, you have to put more *into* the organization. Only people with an entitlement spirit expect to be compensated without producing any new results.

Long-Term Investing:

The next set of investing tools is designed for long-term purposes. There are several options for your long-term investing. Some of the more common tools are private company stocks, real estate, mutual funds, 401k, Roth IRA, etc. I do not claim to be a financial planner, so I will recommend that you secure your own independent financial advisor in your local area to discuss investing. However, I can provide a basic overview of each of the tools mentioned.

Purchase Your Home

It is very likely that your home will be one of the biggest purchases that you will ever make. Owning a home is a dream come true for millions of people. Purchasing a home, whether prior to your new commitment to build wealth or after you began this journey, is critical to long-term wealth building. I didn't mention home ownership earlier in the steps because I wanted you to free yourself from the baggage that you already had. Now that you're free, you will make your home purchase with a different mentality. When you purchase a home to use as your primary residence, you must do so from an investor's point of view. There are several factors to consider: location, location, location! Buying your home in the right location is crucial to a successful purchase. When you're buying a home as a primary residence, you have to ask yourself questions like, *Can I see myself here long term? Can I raise my family here? How do I feel when I drive up to the house? How do I feel as I drive through the neighborhood? How is the access to freeways, grocery stores, and work? How are the schools in the area? Are there a lot of homes on the market in the neighborhood? If there are, why?* These are all subtle things that you need to be thinking about before you invest thousands of dollars into a home. After you find the home you want, negotiate the price with the seller. Trust me, there's always room for negotiation.

Pay Off Your Home

Once you've purchased the home, the next step is to quickly pay it off. I would recommend that a 15-year mortgage be the max that you take out on the house. This way, you can pay substantially less interest to the bank over the life of the loan, and your home will be paid off in 15 years instead of the traditional 30 years. If you can't afford the 15-year loan, do the

30-year loan. However with the 30-year loan, you can still pay it off sooner. By simply taking your one-time monthly payment of, for example, $1,000 and making bi-weekly payments of $500, you will usually cut approximately 6 to 8 years off the loan (depending on the loan balance). By doing bi-weekly payments, you go from making 12 one-time payments a year to 26 payments (remember there are 52 weeks in a year) which not only cuts down on the interest, but also makes one full additional principal payment per year. By paying the mortgage bi-weekly, you are also reducing the loan balance faster, which is reducing the total amount of interest you will pay over the life of the loan. Thus, you will pay off the home at a much faster rate.

Caution: Do not allow a third-party affiliate to set up your bi-weekly payments and charge you a fee to do it. Some banks will do this for free if you have an account with them. If not, you can still set up bi-weekly payments by simply taking your monthly mortgage amount and dividing it by 12. The amount you come up with can simply be added to your full payment each month as additional principal, and effectively, you will have the same results because you will still be paying one full additional payment per year on the loan (ex: $1000/12 = $83.33 extra per month that you would add to the payment totaling $1083.33 per month). By establishing bi-weekly payments and paying additional money each payment towards the principal amount of the loan, you can still pay it like a 15-year mortgage while having the security of a contractual 30-year loan. You would have to call your bank and ask them to work up the numbers to determine how much extra you would have to pay towards the principal in order to pay off the loan in 15 years.

In the event of an emergency or job loss, you can always revert back to the 30-year payment and cut off the extra money going to the principal balance. Having your home paid off and no other debts will have you well on your way to building substantial wealth to enjoy in your lifetime – wealth that you can leave behind as an inheritance for your children and grandchildren.

Private Company Stocks

Large companies use the selling of partial ownership of the company to private investors (you) as a means to grow and expand their business. Basically, they offer individual shares (small, micro portions of ownership) on the stock market, and investors can purchase the shares in exchange for part ownership of the company. In exchange, the private investor benefits from the profits that the company makes. Because the shares are from one company only, the rate of return is typically higher; however the risk is also higher. If the company's worth drops, the share value is directly impacted, dropping with the company.

Mutual Funds

In plain terms, a mutual fund simply means a group of shares from multiple companies that a group of people "mutually" agree to purchase in bulk amounts. As a result, instead of having all of your money in one stock, the mutual fund has multiple stocks from various companies. By purchasing with a group of people, it decreases the risk of you losing all of your money if one stock's value drops substantially. The other funds in the mutual fund group help to avoid a drastic loss all at once. These types of investments are typically considered safer/low-risk, and therefore, the rate of return is normally lower.

Real Estate

At this point, you should have your entire income free, and you should be able to place a large portion of your income in some form of savings account. That money can be used to purchase real estate for cash instead of financing. Financing your primary residence is fine; however, investment real estate should be purchased with cash. Don't fall back into borrowing money! Set a goal to purchase one property a year or every two years depending on your income. I've learned just from my experience that low-to-middle income neighborhoods are more profitable than high-end areas for rental income purposes.

Despite the 2008 housing crisis that caused a ripple effect globally, in my opinion, real estate is still a much better investment than other investment options. Unlike stock, there's always going to be a demand for housing. Our population continues to grow, so housing will always be in demand. Also, while there are a lot of new things being created, there is only a limited supply of land. Thus, my argument is substantiated by the fact that real estate and housing are limited resources in ever-increasing demand. With real estate, you can drive by and touch a tangible asset over which you have a lot of control. You can also personally add value to real estate with improvements, renovations, landscaping, etc.

Before the S&P 500 and the Dow Jones Industrial Average were created, the wealthiest people had real estate in their portfolios as a means of building their wealth. In my opinion, a depressed real estate market is the perfect opportunity to find some great deals on property. Billionaire investor Warren Buffett once said, "When everyone else is greedy, be fearful, and when everyone else is fearful, be greedy." In essence, he was saying to buy low and sell high. Wise investors practice this philosophy frequently.

The problem with the housing crash of 2008 was that too many greedy lenders and overnight real estate investors were inflating the prices of real estate, creating record returns on borrowed money. However, when the market corrected itself, there was a surplus of homes on the market and no one to purchase them because the shady lending practices had finally caught up to the banks and mortgage brokers making the loans. Some people saw this as a disaster, while others who had built a solid foundation with their money saw this as an opportunity. It was like a fire sale! The people who had resisted the impulse purchases and get-rich-quick schemes were able to buy real estate at 30%, 50%, even 70% below their worth!

There are still lots of opportunities in the real estate market for people to build wealth, if done correctly. When purchasing real estate for investment purposes, remember that you make your money when you purchase the property. Never purchase based on potential increase in value because this is beyond your control. An example of this would be to buy in a neighborhood because a developer has plans to build a race track in the area, and housing prices are expected to increase 20% to 30%. That purchase would be unwise because it's contingent on the developer. If, for some unforeseen reason, the developer does not build the track, you're stuck with a house that you may end up taking a financial loss on because you purchased it on a faulty premise.

When you purchase investment property, you should always, always, always make sure that there is enough profit potential in the purchase on the front end at the time of purchase to withstand virtually any situation and that there will still be room for some profit. An example of this would be to purchase a home that is in foreclosure in a neighborhood where the average home sells for $250,000. If you can purchase the home for $150,000 with expectations of spending an additional $20,000 in repairs and renovations, you are virtually guaranteed to still make a profit when you sell the property. If you purchase the property at the right price, it can endure virtually any storm and still come out profitable.

Retirement Savings Accounts

Saving for retirement is crucial to long-term wealth building. Too many people go through life living from paycheck to paycheck, just barely getting by. Since most will never stop to analyze their financial condition, they end up wasting a lifetime of income. By the time reality slaps them in the face as they approach retirement age, it's almost too late to try to start saving; at this point, it is nearly impossible to build enough wealth to sustain them for the remaining years of their lives when they stop receiving a full-time salary from working.

One of the most common retirement investing tools is the IRA. An IRA is an Individual Retirement Account. There are two main IRA plans available. One type is the Traditional IRA, and the other is the Roth IRA. A Traditional IRA is simply an investment tool utilized to save money for retirement on a pre-taxed basis. You can set up a percentage of your income from your salary that will be placed into the investment of your choice, and it's not taxed on the front end (you don't pay taxes on it now). For example, if you make $5,000 a month and you contribute 10% into your Traditional IRA account, this would mean that $500 of your money would go directly into that account towards your retirement. Therefore, you would only have to pay taxes (federal, state, income, etc.) on $4,500 of your salary. That $500 will grow tax-free until you reach retirement age. However, at retirement, you will have to pay taxes on the money you withdraw. In addition to paying taxes on the money you put in, you will also have to pay taxes on the growth earned over the years while the money was accumulating interest from your investments.

A Roth IRA, however, is slightly different. With a Roth IRA, you can contribute the same amount of money from your check as before; however the money you contribute is not tax exempt. In essence, if we used the same salary example, you would pay taxes on the entire $5,000 now while having $500 deducted and contributed to your Roth IRA. The benefit of this type of IRA is that when you withdraw the money at retirement, you won't have to pay any taxes on the initial money you invested or the interest the money earned while it was accumulating over the years.

The deciding factor is this: would you rather pay taxes on $500 per month now (Roth IRA), or would you rather pay taxes on $500 plus the interest earned over your working lifetime later when your income isn't as high (Traditional IRA)? You can make that choice on an individual basis. However, I would recommend the Roth IRA personally, because paying taxes on $500 at today's tax rate is a lot less than paying taxes on the entire savings plus the interest the savings has accumulated over your entire working career. If I have $1,000,000 in my retirement account that I'm drawing $5,000 a month from, the taxes on the $5,000 retirement check will be much higher than the taxes on the $500 I paid up front.

Insurance

This is possibly one of the most overlooked investments around. Unfortunately, when most people think of insurance, they think of a lifelong bill that never goes away. Well, that is true. However, consider your insurance as an investment for your future (not referencing growth savings insurance policies) and the stability of your family. Instead of viewing insurance as an obligation, treat it as a small investment with a guaranteed return. The average person in good health can obtain a term life insurance policy for under $30 a month that will yield over a $500,000 return upon their death (based on the plan chosen).

Even if you paid $30 a month for 30 years, that would only equal a payout of $10,800, while the return on the insurance policy would be $500,000. Do the math! That's a *major* return on investment! I know you're probably saying, *"But I don't get that money... it will be left for my family!"* Exactly! This investment is for the sustainability of your family when you are no longer here to provide for and support them. As I mentioned earlier, none of the things that we have will transition with us when we die, so someone else will benefit from what we leave. What better gift to leave your spouse, children, ministry, favorite charity, etc. than a large lump sum of money to continue your support of them after your death?

Entrepreneurial Endeavors

Many of today's first-generation millionaires earned their wealth by starting a small business that produced a product or service for consumers. This business was likely created as a way to solve a problem or to meet a need for someone. That's the basis of starting a business. Always ask before starting the business: Am I solving a problem or meeting a need? If the answer is *Yes*, then proceed. If the answer is *No*, seriously consider another venture into which you can invest your time and money.

What is an Entrepreneur?

An entrepreneur is a person who organizes and manages a business undertaking, assuming the risk of starting the business for the sake of profit. An entrepreneur is someone who sees an opportunity in the market, develops a plan to start the business, manages the business start-up and ultimately receives the profits from the business. For the sake of this discussion, I will also include an entrepreneur as someone who is a self-employed professional like doctors, attorneys, realtors, dentists, etc.

In order to become effective at entrepreneurship, you must be willing to take some risks. Calculated risks are important to wealth building. Simply saving money alone isn't enough to build substantial amounts of wealth. By investing in entrepreneurial endeavors, you substantially increase the odds of building wealth more quickly than by saving alone.

Entrepreneurial endeavors do to your money what chemically-enhanced steroids do for body builders and athletes: they enhance your efforts and make your results grow bigger, faster, and stronger than normal. Be careful not to confuse legitimate entrepreneurial endeavors with get-rich-quick schemes.

These are two different types of animals! Starting and growing a business usually takes years of work before it ever becomes profitable. As always, there are exceptions to the rule, but generally, business start-ups will not produce instant wealth.

********NEWS FLASH********

I'm still operating from the premise that you are still on track with the fore-mentioned steps. Don't take your money from your emergency fund to start a business! Your emergency fund is dedicated for just what it says: EMER-GENCIES! If you want to start a business, the funds for this should be set aside just as you would save money for any other purchase or venture.

What are some examples of possible entrepreneurial endeavors?

The entrepreneurial endeavor you choose will largely depend on your current skill set or area of expertise. For example, a good friend of mine worked as a sales representative for a pharmaceutical company. Part of his job was to meet with doctors at their clinics and present new products (medications) from his company in hopes that the doctors would prescribe the new drugs to their patients. As he met with the doctors, he would hire a catering company to provide food as a part of the selling process.

Oftentimes, the catering company would be late delivering the food, or the time it would take for him to go and pick up the food wasn't worth the effort. After years of doing this, he suddenly realized that this was a niche market that he could tap into – he would provide the food himself. He quickly developed the business and started using his own company to cater the meals for the doctors that he met with. Further, in addition to his own presentations, he informed his co-workers of the service he provided, and they began to use his company to cater the food for their presentations.

This is an example of identifying a need and tapping into a market that was underdeveloped. As I stated earlier, this individual identified a need and solved a problem. Consequently, he has a successful catering business that is helping him to "pump up" his wealth building efforts.

There are thousands of ways to become an entrepreneur. Opportunities abound when it comes to solving problems and meeting needs. I've thought like an entrepreneur since I was a youth. I remember when I was in high school, my cousin Sarah was a hair stylist and worked at a medium-size hair salon. I started working there as the janitor (sweeping and mopping floors) initially making $25 for the entire day. I saw an opportunity, and I decided to take advantage of a captive audience of women who were getting their hair done (which could take hours).

I asked my cousin if I could solicit business at the salon. I offered to take the women's cars and detail them while they were getting their hair done. The timing was perfect and for them, it was convenient. My sales pitch was "Beautiful women shouldn't drive dirty cars!" It worked like a charm. Since they were clients of my cousin, they trusted me with their vehicles. They were not going anywhere for hours, and the car wash was right around the corner, so it was a win-win situation!

I would charge between $10 and $15 to wash, vacuum, and dress the tires. On average, I would make up to $400 on a Saturday. Of course, I quit my janitorial job. In exchange for allowing me to solicit their clients, I would wash my cousin's car and the salon owner's car for free. While my friends were in the mall "Ooooh shopping" (getting excited about things they couldn't purchase), I was making money. Opportunities are all around us, and they are ready to be tapped into if we have the right perspective. Start looking for opportunities to solve problems and meet needs. It could change your life!

Step #10. Give

Giving is an act of your free will. It usually stems from a desire to help others meet a need. No one can be forced to give, nor is anyone else obligated to give you anything. To truly give, there can be no guilt associated with the giving. When you do give, you should not give with any hidden agendas. The act of giving should be rooted in a genuine care for someone, and the return on your gift should be the joy of being able to help someone else in their time of need. Therefore, when someone gives you something, it is the ultimate gesture of kindness, and the appropriate response should be "Thank You."

Being in a position to give is a favorable position for anyone to be in, for it means that you are not in the opposite position – one in which you need for others to give to you. Having the ability to freely give of yourself and your resources is priceless. At this point in your financial journey, you are capable of making a difference in the lives of others through your giving. You have just become a philanthropist with the ability to give to your favorite organizations and charities as you desire.

Chapter Nine

I'M FINALLY FREE

Congratulations! At this point, you have made the necessary mental adjustments and preparations to continue on your journey of wealth building! You have committed yourself to taking the following steps of the 10-Step Redemption Plan in order to Unlock Your Mind and Unlock Your Money!

Step 1: Establish Your Motive

Step 2: Identify Your Kryptonite

Step 3: Create Some Accountability

Step 4: Make the Commitment to Yourself, to Your Family, and to God

Step 5: Create an Emergency Fund

Step 6: Prioritize Your Budget

Step 7: Pay Off Debt

Step 8: Complete Your Emergency Fund

Step 9: Invest

Step 10: Give

If you have embraced all of the mental keys and incorporated the steps of the 10-Step Redemption Plan into your life, you have successfully Unlocked Your Mind and Your Money! Your mentality can no longer hold you hostage.

I hope that you've enjoyed this book, and I hope that it has been helpful in your life. I pray that the principles that were discussed were not only life-changing for your financial life, but more importantly, I pray that they will be life-changing in your walk with God. If you are a current believer in Jesus Christ as your Lord and Savior, I hope that this book has strengthened your walk and faith in God. I also pray that this book has strengthened your financial life in order for you to be more effective in your support of ministry.

If you are not yet a believer in Jesus Christ, I invite you to examine your life. If you do this, you will surely find that there is a void in your life that can only be filled when you are reconciled back into a proper relationship with God. I invite you to seek out a local ministry in your area that is Bible-centered, Spirit-filled and community-building with a leader who has the heart of God (Jeremiah 3:15). I pray that you will find a ministry that can equip you to do the work of ministry in your area.

IT'S DECISION TIME!

Let me tell you a short story that will help your perspective along the way. The Bible tells the story of the children of Israel, God's chosen people. According to the story, the children of Israel were enslaved in Egypt under the rule of the Pharaoh. However, God desired for His people to be free. Thus He chose a leader, Moses – a man with his own weaknesses – to lead His people out of the bondage of Egyptian slavery and into the Promised Land. God sent Moses to Pharaoh and commanded Pharaoh to let His people go, but Pharaoh resisted, hardening his heart and refused to free the Israelites. However, after God struck Egypt with ten horrible plagues, including killing Pharaoh's first born, Pharaoh finally let the children of Israel go. The Israelites fled in haste.

Shortly thereafter, Pharaoh had a change of heart about letting these people go, and he commanded his army to pursue them in order to kill them. By the time the army neared the children of Israel, the freed people had arrived at the Red Sea, which God miraculously opened in order to let them cross. After each one of the children of Israel had crossed through the sea on dry land, the enemies that pursued them tried to follow them across; however, God closed the sea on top of Pharaoh's army, and Israel's enemies were washed away.

Now that the children of Israel were on the other side of captivity and finally free, they found themselves in the wilderness, and they immediately had a decision to make: continue to move ahead into what

God had promised them or go back to Egypt, the place of bondage. In front of them was the land that God told them they would possess, the Promised Land that flowed with milk and honey (an abundance of resources). Behind them was their former life in Egypt where they were simply slaves.

Initially, they sent several spies to scout out the Promised Land, which was currently inhabited by others. After spying out the land, the spies were to report back to Moses and the people about what they saw. The spies came back with a negative report crying, "We are like grasshoppers in our own sight!" or in modern day language, "We've got to overcome *giants* to get this done! It'll never work!" They were fearful of the obstacles that they saw that separated them from their Promised Land, and they did not believe God despite all of the miracles He had done in delivering them out of bondage and by providing for them in the wilderness.

However, there was another spy named Joshua who had also gone to spy out the land, but his report was quite different. He was confident in what God had promised, and he was ready for the challenge that lay ahead. He realized that what was in front of them in the Promised Land was much better than what was behind them in Egypt. He also knew that his current condition in the wilderness was not favorable either. Unfortunately, the people who had heard the negative report of the spies were persuaded that they would not be able to possess this land that was filled with giants. Why? Because they were fearful! Having an abundance of resources was foreign to this group of former slaves. They did not know how to appreci-ate the blessings of God, so instead of believing God and moving forward to possess their Promised Land, they opted to stay in the wilderness. To make matters worse, they blamed their leader, Moses, for their situ-ation and said silly things like, "We would have been better off had we not left Pharaoh's camp. At least there, we could eat!" Amazingly, they would have preferred to go back into slavery than to put forth a little effort in a fixed fight that God had already won on their behalf.

Ultimately, the people decided that it was too hard to acquire the abundance and wealth that the Prom-ised Land had to offer, even though God Himself said that He would give it to them. They decided to stay where they were most comfortable (in poverty, broke, in debt, etc.) – in the wilderness. Consequently, God had to allow that entire generation to die before He could use Joshua (the spy with the favorable report who believed that they were well able to take the land) to lead the next generation into the Promised Land.

What will you decide? Will you embrace the prin-ciples in this book and be encouraged like Joshua to go and possess all that God has for you, or will you take the position of others and say that it's too hard to change? Will you conclude that you're going to stay in your comfort zone, because in doing so, at least you know what you're working with here in poverty? What will it be? Will the money you've spent on this book be another bad investment? As the author, I certainly hope not!

MY PERSONAL PRAYER FOR YOU

I'm a firm believer in the power of prayer, and I'm convinced that my God hears my prayers. I feel as if I've just had a conversation with you as you read through this book and learned about my past failures, successes, near death experiences and financial mishaps. It is my hope that my story can help you to avoid the mistakes that I've made. In order to reduce the likelihood of you having to deal with the pain I suffered through, I would like to say a prayer to God on your behalf:

God, I thank You for the opportunity to write this book. I thank You for the wisdom found in Your Word. I thank You for the experiences that I've been through and the mistakes that I've made. God, You orchestrated those mistakes that gave me the motive to seek You and find out how You want us, as believers, to manage Your resources.

Now God, I thank You for the readers of this book. I pray that Your favor will be upon them as they embark on this new endeavor of financial liberation. I ask that You would bless their efforts as they walk through the 10-Step Redemption Plan. God, I pray that You would be right there with them each step of the way, for I know that You are the ultimate accountability partner. Lord, as they get closer to the final steps, I pray that You will always bring back to their remembrance what the ultimate goal of this process is, which is to free themselves from the bondage and limitations of their financial restrictions in order to become available to be used by You in order to expand the influence of Your kingdom. Lord, I know that it may become intoxicating for them to become someone who goes from having very little to having great wealth, but I pray that You would set parameters on their life by which they are bound. God, I know that You will not violate their individual free moral agency or ability to choose and make them do anything. But I pray that the process which was laid out and the foundation that was laid in the beginning was effective enough to keep them grounded as they enjoy the new liberty of being free from debt and having money in the bank at their disposal. Most importantly God, I pray that You would touch the person who is reading this book that does not have a relationship with You. Reveal Yourself to them in a real way. Give them a burning desire to seek You and to serve in Your kingdom.

Just as they will have to ignore the commentary from friends and family in this transition to wealth building, God, let them keep in mind that they will be better off than they were before and that the opinions of their friends and family will not get them to a place of financial freedom. Help them to understand that this relationship with You is of even greater significance than money will ever be, for this relationship with You is dealing with their eternity.

God, I pray for those who are going to come to know You through this book and other books to come from me. And now God, I ask that your protection would be upon the reader of this book and that Your blessings will overtake them so that they, too, can be a witness of how absolutely AWESOME YOU ARE! AMEN.

A FEW FINAL COMMENTS TO MY FELLOW BELIEVERS IN CHRIST

The next few pages are directed to those who are committed believers in Jesus Christ – those who share my faith. However, I encourage everyone to continue to read on to the end.

While many accumulate abundant material possessions and wealth for their own personal greed and consumption, believers should be focused upon accumulating abundant wealth so that they can be used by God to touch the lives of people all over the world. When God hand-selects a chosen people to execute and represent His will on earth, He always provides the resources that are needed to bring it to manifestation. If we apply His principles of financial stewardship, we will be in position to receive a steady flow of God's resources. These resources are not for us to consume; instead we are to manage the resources based on the instructions and guidance of the owner of all things – God! As we discussed earlier in the book, God is the true owner of all that we have, and therefore we must consult with Him on how to distribute His resources.

If we as a body of believers could collectively get our finances in order and get into a position that would allow us to give freely without consulting with our master (Debt) first, we would be able to truly expand the influence of God's kingdom across the world. Our ministries would be able to do more concerning the preaching of the gospel of the kingdom. We could send missionaries into rural parts of the world to share the love of God with people who are cut off from the rest of society.

Further, when we begin to operate with financial soundness, I truly believe that our ministers could actually get back to teaching the gospel in its original context without manipulating the scriptures in order to please a money-hungry people. I'm convinced that there are a lot of pastors and church leaders that have sold out to preaching a gospel of prosperity, even though they did not originally start off with ambitions of "pimping the church". Instead, they succumbed to the pressure to take this route due to the demands of a people who demonstrated that having a relationship with God by way of Jesus Christ was not enough for them; they wanted God to do more for them. They wanted God to make them rich. These people really act as if salvation and having eternal life with God is not enough, and they are determined to live their best life NOW! Somehow they have been convinced to believe that they can force God to bless them by turning His scriptures against Him and reminding Him that He is now bound by His Word.

If we would only come together and stop chasing after what Satan, the god of this world offers (money, fame, status, power, etc.), and if we would begin to chase after God's purpose for our lives, we would see the power of God manifested throughout the world. Instead, we have been blinded by the god of this world, and our daily pursuit is centered on getting money with wrong motives and on satisfying the cravings of our fleshly desires.

God commands us in Matthew 6:33, "But seek first the kingdom of God and His righteousness, and all these things shall be added to you." A few verses earlier, in Matthew 6:24, Jesus says, "No one can serve two masters; for either he will hate the one and love the other, or else he will be loyal to the one and despise the other. You cannot serve God and mammon (money)."

Kingdom-focused believers do not seek to serve money; instead, we desire to use money as a tool to help us to be available to God and to serve others on behalf of God.

The question is often asked, "What is the difference between a non-believer building wealth and a believer building wealth?" My response is simple. Intent and motivation! Believers build wealth to be *used by* God, while non-believers build wealth in order to *be like* God. Believers give out of good intentions, just as God gives to them, while non-believers give out selfishness, always wanting to know "What's in it for me?"

If you really want to be used by God, start giving of your resources in order to share the love of God with your neighbors, co-workers, family, associates, and strangers abroad. That my friends, is the true purpose for building wealth! God bless you on your journey!

ABOUT THE AUTHOR

Derrick Love was born in Lake Providence, LA and was raised by a single parent along with five other siblings. While the expectations for success were dismal in the environment in which he was raised, he was determined not to allow his environment to dictate his future. Dealing with adversity as a young minority became a way of life, but instead of giving in and becoming a statistic, he decided this was not going to be the end of the story for his life. As a teenager, he began to pursue ways to escape his current environment in Louisiana and was afforded the opportunity to move to Houston, TX to live with relatives.

Driven by fear, and determined to not become another member of the status quo for young black boys, he pursued many ventures in entrepreneurship while learning various skills and trades. In high school, he created GUGOGS, an acronym for "Get Up, Get Out, Get Something." After graduating high school, he joined the military and served for over five years in the U.S. Navy. While actively serving in the military, Derrick partnered with his cousin Jerome Love and GUGOGS was transformed from a "personal mental driver" into a full line of clothing including t-shirts, hats, and sweaters to be shared with the world. GU-GOGS has taken many forms since its inception, and the most recent forum birthed from GUGOGS is the Texas Black Expo which was founded by Jerome Love. Fueled with new information and exposure to the business world, Derrick was even more determined to live the life he had only been able to dream about.

After quickly promoting through the ranks in the military, Derrick's entrepreneurial drive would not allow him to settle for the military and its glass ceiling. While trying to determine his next move, he became exposed to Pastor Dana Carson who at the time had a thriving ministry in Austin, TX but was in transition to Houston, TX to relocate his ministry headquarters. After hearing the powerful messages from Dr. Carson, he decided the next phase of his life would be centered around the Word of God he preached. He returned to Houston and bought his first rental property which was a four-plex. While living in one of the units and renting the other three in order to pay the mortgage, Derrick decided to obtain his real estate license. His real estate business became very successful and his income sky rocketed. It was in this season that the real lessons on finances began to be taught with clarity.

To book Derrick Love for speaking engagements, book signings, or guest appearances, please submit your requests to:

Email: info@derrickjlove.com
Social Media:
www.facebook.com/unlockyourmoney
Website: www.derrickjlove.com